Books by the Author

My Journey to Peace with PTSD
BEe Perspective Beekeeping
Apitherapy – From a Beekeeper's Perspective

My Life's Crazy Quilt

Lady Spirit Moon Cerelli, Author

Copyrighted 2025

All rights reserved by Lady Spirit Moon Cerelli. Printed and bound in the United States of America. The editorial arrangement, analysis, and professional commentary are subject to this copyright notice. No portion of this book may be copied, retransmitted, reposted, duplicated, or otherwise used without the express written approval of the author, except by reviewers who may quote brief excerpts in connection with a review. United States laws and regulations are public domain and not subject to copyright. Any unauthorized copying, reproduction, translation, or distribution of any part of this material without permission by the author is prohibited and against the law.

Biography, Memoirs

ISBN-13: 978-0-9798883-6-6

Book cover design by Lady Spirit Moon Cerelli

I dedicate this book to those I have met on my life's journey. To those who taught me lessons that allowed me to grow and expand my knowledge of the world; thereby giving me knowledge of myself. I will even go so far as to dedicate the book to the eight brothers and sisters, with whom I no longer have contact, and the one with whom I still communicate. They, too, taught me lessons I would not have experienced in any other way other than through a sibling. I learned to take what is termed "bad experiences" and turned them into lessons and looked upon the good experiences as blessings. I have garnered from both before letting them go; to not only loving myself, but to even like the person I have become. I thank all of you.

MY LIFE'S CRAZY QUILT

by

Lady Spirit Moon Cerelli

Table of Contents

Introduction 1
PART I – My Youth 5
    I Arrive 7
    Surrogacy 9
    Second Trauma 10
    We Move into Our New House 12
    The Little Woman 13
    I Grew Up 22
    Gossip 25
    Junior High 26
    Learning About the Silence 29
    High School 31
    Music Room 33
    Senior Year 35
PART II - Navy 39
    Navy Recruit 41
    Learning Movement in an Altered State 46
    Liberty to Home 48
    IBM School 49
    Charleston, SC 52
    Black Button First Appears 54
    AWOL 56
    Captain's Mast 60
    Civilian Life 63
    Home – Not Exactly 65

PART III – Married Life 71
Married and Pregnant 73
The Maternal Instinct 75
Roger - Our First Foster Child 76
Gil and Other Teens 80

PART IV – Empty Nest 87
Always Moving 89
A Different Altered State 89
Journeying 92
Cerelli's Herb Farm & Store 94
Two Deaths 99
Buddy 105
Life Goes On 111
Unexpected Blessing 114

PART V – New Beginning 119
Sneedville, Tennessee 121
Being Hard 123
Surreal Life 125
Counseling Again 126
Changing My Tune 128
The Accident 130
More Spiritual Doors Open 131
Court Hearing 133

PART VI – Life Reveals Itself 137
Flashback 139
North Carolina 144
Healing 148

Beekeeping	150
PART VII – Living the Life	**155**
Terre Madre International Festival	157
Travels from 2011 through 2013	161
Senegal, Africa, 2011	162
Toulouse, France, October, 2011	165
Senegal, Africa, May and October, 2013	169
A Different Attitude	176
Getting Ready	179
Separation	184
Grieving	186
A New Me	188
Japan, Senegal & Uganda	190
Something Different	196
Still Learning	198
PART VIII – Am I Done?	**201**
Who AM I	202
Living Well	204

Introduction

Every summer in my youth I stayed with my aunt and cousins for a few weeks. Aunt Helen had a neighbor who seemed to be as old as the hills, with a farm located the end of the road a few hundred feet away from her driveway. I would watch him walk from his house to the barn, usually talking to an invisible friend. I visited him often. His strange personality fascinated me because he always responded to my questions with an enigmatic response or a grunt. Sometimes his comments would pique my curiosity. One day, while in his barn watching him milk a cow, he stood up from his milking stool, straightened his back, and said, "Life's a journey."

I loved his conversations, even though I didn't understand a lot of them. I knew this was a good opportunity to get one started. Eagerly, I asked, "What does that mean?"

He looked off into the far distance with his glistening eyes and responded, "Imagine driving in a truck on a strange road. Atter a while you come to the end of a lane. You don't know how ya got there, but ya knows you gotta back up all the way outta there to get back to where ya went in – all the while looking behind you. Ya knew you was daydreamin' and it almost got ya into trouble. Once on the road again, you keep drivin' 'cause something inside o' you says ya gotta keep agoin'. You find yourself drivin' on different pathways, different roads or lanes, biggins and littlins, because folks steered ya thatta way. You get mad at yourself because ya think ya knowed better." He stood up and picked up the milk bucket, then stared at me like he was wondering when I had gotten there.

He took a deep breath and started his slow walk toward the house, me following alongside. "So, where did I go and when do I stop driving?" I was really curious.

He continued, "You drive o'er obstacles and small bumps in the road, sometimes wonderin' what they is, but they's no time to look at 'em. You meet folks. Sometimes you stop 'n talk. Sometimes you go off the road. Sometimes it takes a while to get back to the main road. Sometimes it is hard drivin' at all. Each day passes, and ya find yourself thinkin' you shoulda done more, done somethin' different, or gone a different way."

We arrived at the bench next to the tree near the front porch of the house. He put his bucket on the ground then sat down. When I got onto his lap, I felt his strong, bony arms automatically wrap around my shoulders. As much as I enjoyed being embraced, which was a novel in my youth, I needed to get to the end of the story. "How long do I drive?"

No longer looking into the distance, he looked down at me with his rheumy eyes and, with a soft smile, tenderly said, "Child, you don't drive."

Sometimes he forgot where he was and what he was talking about. "You were telling me a story about me driving a truck down the road," I reminded him.

"Ah, the journey. Yes, child. Everyone travels down a different road through life. Everyone has troubles. But they's always someone or somethin' around to help ya. Life can be hard, tender, funny, and full o' sorrow. The key is to keep a movin'. Eventually you get on the right road again."

We got up from the bench and moved toward the house. "But when do I stop driving?"

He stared at me for a moment as though he couldn't believe I had asked the question. "Why, child, you stop when you die."

―――

I'm 82 years old and often that conversation would haunt me like a whisper coming out of the corner of my mind, wandering around in my brain, pushing slowly and gently off from one side then across to the other as I contemplated his words. I would often ponder on that road of life and wonder a lot at how I got to where I was in that moment. I can still hear his soft, tender voice, and see his lean, bony frame walking toward me from the barn. He was right, of course. I did drive a truck. But often my life's journey felt more like I was on the back of a stubborn mule, and many times I had to get off and pull it or push it along. On rare occasions, I would walk alongside that stubborn mule.

When I related stories of my experiences, people would often tell me to write a book about my life. I laughed at the idea, because I didn't think it interesting enough. Recently, when I heard myself relating a story about one of my international travels, I thought ... "Maybe." My life has been unusual from to being a surrogate to my nine siblings starting at the age of four; to incest at seven years old; into the Navy where I was sexually assaulted multiple times and lost three months of my memory; diagnosed with severe PTSD and survived; married for 53+ years and survived; fostered teenagers and survived; kept bees that taught me my humanity; traveled internationally; authored three books; was an ambassador for a research center; journalist; created a website.... I have been told that my life is like a crazy quilt, needing to be looked at, into, and understood – with each piece teaching me a lesson, as it is placed into a timeframe of my life.

Life would teach me that there are experiences that need to happen for us to learn the lessons involved. And when the lessons have been learned or the relationship has fulfilled its purpose, we would leave them behind. I would think of these experiences, and of what I have learned from them. I had also grasped the idea that if you don't heed or learn the lessons, they revisit you.

Early on, I learned to look into things differently than the way most people saw them. I would view a situation from its back door and peer *into* the situation rather than at it. For many years I thought it strange that others didn't do this. But it would finally occur to me that abuse can cause the brain to view "*into*" a thing, looking for a reason or an excuse to run or try to understand what is happening. This helped me to keep from being blindsided by looking at what the situation or person wanted me to see. Eventually, I termed this to be "left-sided" thinking, meaning the opposite of right-sided or forward thinking, as is considered normal thinking.

Religion was too restrictive for me, with rules on how to honor God, whom I call Guidance. As I walked my life's journey and being 98% Celtic, I was born with certain gifts that revealed themselves early. But it took a canoe accident to actually open the door to the spirit world. Years afterward, I would learn of my other gifts as their need arose. I had always thought myself weird or different from most people. But once my gifts became known, I was told I was gifted. My spiritual world not only taught me my life's lessons, but showed me a Universe far grander and more expansive than most humans know.

My adventurous life actually began when I was 62, and I wandered into my local post office. Walk with me as I write about the most extraordinary creature that has existed for millions of years before humans. Read how I become obsessed with the honeybee and their community as they help me become a healthy human being in body and mind, and connect with all things spiritual. Learn how they taught me compassion, acceptance over forgiveness, to love and honor everything and everyone, and to generously give back. Most importantly, learn how they taught me a part of my humanity I had never known before.

Know You Are Loved
Lady Spirit Moon

PART I

My Youth

I Arrive

Mountain-bred, I was mountain-born on April 6, 1944, in the Appalachia Mountains of Kentucky when my mother, Lillian Marie Williams, was fifteen-and-a-half and named me, Emma Diona Williams. Emma was my grandmother's name. Diona was the name of a young girl in a book my mother was reading while in the hospital just before giving me birth. I learned in my adult life that Diona is Hawaiian-Portuguese, derived from the Goddess Diana, Warrior of Women and Children. That name would be appropriate, for when I became an adult I would advocate for women and children. My mother told me her uncle threatened to take me away from her for the monthly welfare check, so she and I went to live with her aunt, whom everyone called Granny. I remember Granny always being on the short side, looking old and wrinkly, always smelling of the peppermint snuff she often dipped, with a Coke bottle in her hand for the spittle. Granny always smiled and showed me how a hug felt while she said, "I love you."

Me, mom, and Moss, 1944

I was considered a bastard child and would never know my biological father. When I was a year old, mom and I rode the train to Monroe, Michigan, where she married Moss Webb. I have no idea how they met, but do remember being told he was in the Army during WW11. He was good looking in his uniform. Too bad that he was a mean alcoholic. Children are born with the innate idea that the parents will love them and not harm them.

Diona age 4

When I was four years old, Moss was very aggressive while undressing me, spending a lot of time taking off my panties and playing with my pee-pee. It had hurt, and I cried. He tossed my body in my own bed and told me to shut up. I don't remember where mom was. With my head under the blanket, I laid in bed sobbing. I think it was more out of shock and hurt feelings than from physical pain. Through the opened window next to my bed, I heard someone say, "Diona, you can do whatever you want." This confused me because I didn't know I wanted to do anything. I had never wondered where the voice came from or who it was. But from that day forward, if I wanted to attempt something, I usually succeeded because it never occurred to me that I couldn't. The purple snow suit Moss gave later was meant to be a peace offering.

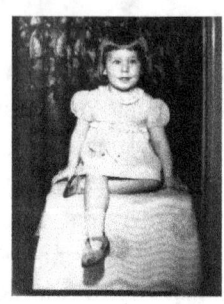

Diona age 6

I learned at an early age to distrust what I was told because my parents, for reasons of their own, often lied to me about anything and everything. I never understood the purpose of lying because they were often of things that could be proven within minutes of telling the lie. I am sharing this because some of what I write may be things my parents have told me and may not be true. From what I understand, we moved into an apartment at 710 E. 4th St. in Monroe after mom and Moss married. I don't remember for how long we stayed there. I really don't remember anything of that time. Though, my future mother-in-law, living on E. 6th Street at that time, told me she remembered me when I was a child.

The Newport Naval Air Station near Monroe, Michigan, changed into many things from the first air station and prisoner of war camp in WWII; to the Newport Nike Missile Base; to the Airport Community Schools; then the training facility for the National Guard. At some point, some of the buildings on the base were known as Darinton apartments. I don't remember when we moved into the middle of one of the long, single floor apartment buildings in the middle of the development. But I still remember our 1611 Virginia Court address.

Me and Elain, my best friend, in homemade sun outfits

The long single-floor barracks had been converted into thirteen apartments per building. Each 24 x 24 apartment had two bedrooms, one small bathroom, and a kitchen-living-dining room combined. An alley ran between the backs of two buildings, with a coal bin for each apartment that no longer held coal, but were often used as storage or for children's hideouts while playing. One vehicle per apartment was allowed to park alongside the coal bin. The building fronts faced each other with large lawn spaces between them. Our yard was fenced in due to the six young children in our family.

Our grade school classes were held in a Quonset hut located about a thousand feet from our apartment. There were sixteen kids in my kindergarten class, where I experienced my first public humiliation. I needed to go to the bathroom and raised my hand but was not allowed to leave. I had peed my pants and cried with my forehead on my folded arms on my desk. I don't remember anything after that incident.

For most of my life, that would be the norm for me – not remembering much after a trauma or painful incident until long afterward. If the trauma is not dealt with by sharing with someone, the ego will protect itself by setting the trauma aside and create a behavior disorder. Sharing one's trauma is a life tool of survival, and one I never learned until I was an adult.

Surrogacy

My brother, Bobby, was born two years after me, followed by my twin sisters, Linda and Jeri, less than a year later. Suzette, Bonnie, and Penny were less than a year apart. All of us slept in the same bedroom. The girls slept three to a double bed with Bobby in a child's cot. When I was seven, we had five in diapers at one time for about two and a half months. Imagine the diapers on two clothes lines, strung between the coal bin and apartment building, full twice a week at a time when only cloth diapers were used. Mom had to have had a scrubbing board in the kitchen sink because we had no washing machine.

When I was four years old, Bobby cried loudly, because his diaper needed to be changed. So, I changed it. I had watched mom do it, and thought I had done it the same way. It was my first time and had put the pin through the diaper and through his skin. I had not yet learned how to use my finger behind the pin to protect the diaper wearer. He screamed for what seemed a long time, until mom investigated and repinned it. She then turned and cussed at me for not changing the diaper correctly. Hurt, I screamed back, "Somebody had to change it." And that began my role as surrogate for my siblings.

My parents always seemed to be mad at each other. They either argued or were silent; a silence that often cut the air and made us kids uncomfortable. So, we made ourselves scarce and played outside as much as possible. They never spoke of love nor never hugged us; didn't say anything to us, unless it was an order to do something or to stop doing something. I grew up thinking that all families were like ours, that we were normal.

Dad drank a lot. There was never enough money, so mom worked as a barmaid. She worked from evening into the early AM hours closing the bar/restaurant. While she worked, daddy would often display cruel stunts; like putting a cat in a pan of water, and telling us he was going to cook it to eat. We would all scream, "No," and start crying. At some point, I became anesthetized to his behavior and thought him stupid. Thinking back on this, it may have been when I started feeling less emotions rather than getting angry. Eventually, I just turned them off.

Second Trauma

When I was seven, daddy was in a truly drunken state when he succeeded in victimizing me. After taking me to his bed for the third time, mom came home early from work and found us in their bedroom. She angrily grabbed my arm, tossed me on the floor, and said, "Get to your own bed." I was scared. Mom had never treated me like that before and ran to my bed hearing their angry argument, with mom using cuss words I had never heard from her. Silence. Then a drawer was yanked open and shut with such a bang, I jumped.

I was a precocious child and had to know what was going on. My heart still racing, I slid out of my bed. Crawling on all fours to the opened door, I poked my head around the thin wall separating our bedrooms. In the darkness, their silhouettes were shown against the window that was lit by the outside street light. Mom had daddy's gun pointed at him, saying, "You touch her again, I will kill you." Daddy said, "Ok. I will leave. But I will be back." The next day, thinking she was on my side, I told mom that daddy had done. She told me it was a nightmare, and that I should forget about it. I was shocked. Why would she think I would lie about a thing like that. After that, the lonely days dragged on as I grew quieter, thinking I was crazy.

For most of my life, I never understood how I could coldly leave a relationship or a situation and not go back until I remembered that scene of the two silhouettes in front of the window. It didn't matter the length or depth of the relationship, or the situation. Once I decided to leave it, I didn't give it another thought. Most often it was because the individual had lied to me. Daddy's statement of leaving was the reason I adopted the attitude that once I left a thing, going back was never an option. I guess I didn't remember his statement of coming back.

He didn't come around much after that gun incident. Mom told me years later that she had to go to his work place to get his check, because there was no food in the house. I don't remember a babysitter, though surely her friend, Mabel, watched us when mom went to work. I remember making oatmeal for breakfast occasionally when mom overslept. I became accustomed to mom's absence and took on more chores to occupy my time and numb my brain. My fatiguing life aged me early.

My memory is hazy regarding this part of my life. But I do remember being not quite eight years old and playing under a lit lamp. I turned to mom and said matter-of-factly, "Daddy's dead." She stopped in mid-motion of lighting a cigarette, gave me a strange look, but remained quiet. About an hour later, the police showed up and told mom that daddy had died in an auto accident. It was a day or two later before mom said anything to me about the cops at the door. I am certain she was wondering how I knew. About forty years would go by before mom would share that her side of the family had intuitive abilities. She was surprised that I had shown them when I was seven.

When daddy died, mom was pregnant with my seventh sibling. Soon after Michael was born, we moved to 712 Adams St. into a 3-bedroom house. The largest bedroom belonged to the girls with three beds. The smallest bedroom belonged to the boys with two beds. Mom had the middle-sized bedroom. The house had a large kitchen, dining room and living room. The fenced back yard was also large, with a one-car garage. Mom and I had an unusual relationship. She talked to me as if I were an adult, but treated me like I was a child. I would balk at this. But at some point, after the seventh sibling came into the world, things changed. I don't remember when or why. Perhaps it was relief on her part after we moved into a larger house. As I understood it, mom received money for each of my siblings through Moss's military service, and was made our guardian through the court system. Those checks went toward house payments and food. I had been told he was my father, so it never occurred to me to ask why no money was received on my behalf. Moss's death actually made life better for us. For a while, we were content.

Whenever I looked at Granny, I had often wondered why she looked so different. In my adulthood, I learned that we were part Melungeon, a mixture of Native American, Turkish and negro heritage. Her hair was similar to a black person's hair. Granny was the one who hugged us and said, "I love you" when she visited two or three times a year. Being hugged as well, I often wondered why mom was never affectionate. Granny's hugs taught me how good it felt to be embraced. Hearing "I love you" always gave me a warm feeling. As an adult, it was cathartic for me to hug another, whenever they would allow, and always told them "I love you." It felt good when giving hugs. Often, folks surprised me with looks of gratitude or blushed cheeks, especially from the men. Thinking on it, I wondered if needing to feel good at that time was the reason I gave the hugs so that I could as much, if not more, than the person I hugged.

Granny in our kitchen

We Move into Our New House

My eight siblings

About two years after we moved into our new house, mom got married. Six months later, she gave birth to my eighth sibling, Harold Davis Junior, nicknamed Davy. My new stepfather was also an alcoholic. He worked during the day as an auto mechanic and body man and drank his beer at night. On the weekends, he would often start drinking his whiskey with beer soon after breakfast. On Sundays, he slept late, and the girls would take their showers while he slept. I learned years later that it was because he had opened the shower curtain on each of my sisters; as he did on me when I was twenty. Mom was aware of this but said or did nothing.

Mom and dad

Dad had roast beef; we had leftover hash. He had steaks; we had soup made from the leftover steak bones. He ate in the kitchen and insisted on his three pieces of silverware be laid out like in a restaurant. Because dad didn't like noises while he ate, the rest of us ate in the dining room an hour before he came home. We sat on chairs with round back supports and vinyl seat covers obtained from the remodeled restaurant/bar where mom had worked. At least the chairs matched. There was an antique highboy in the dining room; my inheritance when mom passed away. Mom purchased whatever furniture we needed from the salvation army store.

Somewhere between the ages of nine and eleven, I remember cleaning all of the cans, boxes, cartons, anything mom had used in the kitchen, and stored them in the basement. This took a while to collect, since we did a lot of scratch cooking. After I knew I'd had enough, I placed a four-foot board on boxes and placed my toy cash register at the end of the makeshift store counter. A shelf unit at the beginning of the counter was where I had placed my "groceries." I gave everyone Monopoly money to spend in my store. I was proud. After a few days, dad said he thought the whole thing was stupid and said so. I tore it down with numbed feelings. Mom said nothing. Unbeknownst to me, my retail experience would set me up for a real store in my future.

Derogatory remarks were common. Stupid was the usual word and stopped us from doing a lot of things that would have made us feel good. When I was eleven, I thought it creative to have my siblings do various things like sing, dance, do acrobatics, and such, and put on a show for the neighborhood and charge a penny. We were having fun. In the middle of it all, I came in from the back yard after we were practicing and told dad what we were doing. He said, "No one is going to want to pay a penny to watch a bunch of stupid kids." That took care of that. I did not say anything to mom about it and learned not to share things with him.

I came to the conclusion that he said things while we felt good just to make us feel bad. It usually worked. Eventually, I learned not to share with mom, as well. There are no more memories of anything else created after that, but do remember starting to roam away from home during this time of my life.

The Little Woman

In the summer of my tenth birthday, I experienced a great loss. One summer day, venturing around the block to the opposite corner, I noticed a yard with a lot of flowers. I peered over the hedge and looked into the face of a fairy-like little woman, not too much taller than I. She surprised me with her child-like face smiling back at me. Reaching her hand over the hedge, she walked me to the gate and invited me into her yard. Opening the gate, she started in by introducing me to her flowers and the little statues of various small animals. Her animated, bubbly personality fascinated me and made me chuckle at times. My sound of my laughter startled me, and I realized that I hadn't laughed much.

Touching some of the flowers in the little woman's garden evoked images of the satin I was not allowed to touch during the rare times when mom and I shopped for sturdy cotton at the fabric store. Walking around in her garden, the little woman taught me awareness of the lines in the rose petals and their velvet softness. She showed me the fine hair on the leaves of other plants and the stiff vein supporting each leaf. I wanted desperately for time to stand still, as I immersed myself into a world where it was just me, my teacher, and her undivided attention. I loved the little woman's patient voice and her small lips, always smiling. I had never before met an angel, and wondered why I cried as I reached up and smeared away a tear, leaving behind a dirty streak.

A lot of her teaching was done with gestures as well as spoken words, because somehow, she knew I couldn't hear well. I had learned to look at people's lips to make out what they were saying. I could hear sounds, but couldn't always make out the words. Later, one of my teachers would discover my hearing loss. The Lions Club paid for the Mastoid surgery on my right ear. As an adult, I would give twenty dollars whenever I saw them ringing for donations, and donated to their medical closets.

By the time we got to the little woman's house, I smelled a sweet, spicy aroma wafting through her screen door, and she gestured a drinking motion. Smiling, I followed and stepped up into her small kitchen. It welcomed me with its tiny table covered with a red-and-white checkered tablecloth and black-and-white tiled floor. I looked at the white counters, the short, squared icebox, and the small four-burner gas stove. *I wonder if this was how all little people lived.* My cheeks were aching a little from smiling so much. Another reminder of how little joy I experienced in my youth.

Slowly, I turned in a slow circle with one hand clasped over the other on top of my head. *Do not touch that, young lady!* I spied a small cupboard containing dishes almost as small as play dishes. They were ornately painted with tiny red and pink flowers and gold-trimmed edges. The cups were sitting inside their matching saucers, slightly larger plates standing on edge behind them, and a matching teapot. All the chinaware was sitting on a lace doily that spilled over the shelf displaying its crocheted edge. These would be the dishes we used for our "teas."

During the next several weeks, visiting a few days a week, I learned she had traveled the world. We would pretend to travel to different countries through our afternoon "teas" with cookies in the flowered dishes; she having tea and me having hot chocolate. The little woman was my escape from my own house, siblings ... all that depressed me.

One day I saw Mom leave the little woman's house and walk in the opposite direction I was traveling, and I was scared. I hid behind the bushes until she was out of sight. *No, Mom. She's mine. I don't want to share her.* The little woman was my special angel. I knew I was being selfish in keeping her to myself, but I just couldn't talk to anyone about her. I was afraid if I did, I wouldn't be able to visit her, or she would just disappear. Neither Mom nor the little woman ever said anything; nor did I see Mom at the house of flowers again.

Spending as much time as I could with her and her garden, I learned how to care for them as well as how to touch with consciousness, to listen, not only to the sounds of the wind and the birds, but to the silence as well. I learned to discern and separate scents and fragrances in my head, as they passed across and through my nose. The little woman embraced me often. Her hugs were deliberate, firm, yet gentle. She loved me by smiling at me when she handed me my hot chocolate; by listening intently with occasional pointed questions when I related stories of my family. Always, there was a warm, soft fuzzy feeling whenever she was near.

Finding her asleep on the couch one day nearly scared me out of my mind. I shook her hard. "Lord, child, you'll push me through the couch," she said, smiling until she saw the expression on my face. "Honey, I'm fine. I was just tired."

"I was scared. You aren't supposed to get sick," I said in a shaky voice, my hands trembling. My fear seemed unreasonable and, for the first time in my life, I found myself relying upon someone as one would rely upon an immovable rock.

The little woman rose from the sofa, explaining, "Ed, my neighbor next door, hasn't been feeling well, and I've been keeping an eye on him until his family gets here."

"Is he alright?" I asked, my hand touching her floral apron. We were at the kitchen sink where she ran water into her teakettle for tea and hot chocolate.

We talked like two people having a conversation, not like one being a child and the other an adult. I knew I could ask the little woman anything. "That's making you sick too. I don't want you sick. I wouldn't know how to take care of you," I flatly stated, wiping away a tear as I went to my chair at the table.

She stopped setting the table and looked at me in my chair. "Young one, my friend needs God's hands, and I intend to give them to him."

I stopped eating my cookie and stared at her. *Sometimes that woman can say the most outlandish things.* "How can you give him God's hands when they are attached to God?" I shook my head. *She can be so silly.* My voice must have sounded incredulous, because she silently dropped down into her chair. Placing her hands in her lap, she studied me. I felt she saw right through to my soul, examining my brain, looking at every one of my cells.

We both jumped when the whistling teakettle shattered the silence.

Getting up, the little woman slowly brought the teakettle to the table, looking like she was throwing all manner of thoughts around in her head. She remained silent as she poured the water into my cup and into her teapot with the teabag in it. She then placed the teapot on the trivet, covered it with a tea cozy. Still silent, she put the kettle back on the stove. Coming back to the table, she absentmindedly stirred my hot chocolate. *Does she think I can't stir it anymore?* I stared at her, wondering if she was okay. After a few more moments she sat down in her chair and peered at me before asking, "What do you know of God?"

I stopped swinging my legs and put cookie in the plate. I always ate my cookies slowly, savoring them. It was my turn to put my hands in my lap. I knew by her tone of voice and the deep silence that followed, that this was important. Even the clock in the living room seemed to stop ticking; as if it, too, waited for my answer.

"I know that God loves me, and that if I don't behave, He will punish me." And then quickly added, "If the devil doesn't get me first." I sat silently for a brief moment before saying. "You know, with both of them after me, I used to be afraid to do anything." Leaning forward, I whispered in a conspiratorial voice, "And sometimes I would do things just to see what they would do. And you know what? Nothing happened." I leaned back in my chair, feeling quite satisfied with myself.

She smiled and said, "That's because God wishes us to be well and happy. He doesn't want to hurt us nor wish us harm." There was a pause before she spoke again. "Folks say that in the beginning there was a big bang, and the universe grew from that, expanding every day. Out of the big bang came all the little sparks of God, and these sparks, too, grow and expand every day."

In my ten-year-old mind, I had a picture of this huge man pointing a gun at the sky and pulling the trigger. Puzzled, I said, "I don't understand. Why would God shoot a gun?"

Chuckling, she responded, "Actually, it was a big explosion of sorts. It's a little difficult to explain because we don't have the words to describe it. Know this: Everything existing in this whole, wide universe," she made a broad outward sweep of her arms, "is God. He's everything, everywhere, at all times."

I looked at my half-eaten cookie, my eyes widening in fear. "Did I just eat God?"

Softly laughing, she said, "Yes, I guess you did." I was on the verge of crying, when she bent over to hug me "Honey, it's okay. Let me explain it another way. God made everything that exists. But everything is made of energy and matter that constantly moves. Nothing dies. It just changes. Everything made of matter goes back to the earth and its energy or essence go back to its origin and becomes another part of the Universe. Can you understand that?"

"Uh-huh," I responded, nodding my head before looking at my good-tasting cookie. *God is a good cook.* I didn't really understand at the moment what she was saying, but I believed her. This conversation never left me, and I would totally understand much later in life.

"He even made our souls, which can also be called the spark of God, or the light of God." She thought for a moment before continuing. "Because everything came from God, you could say all things are tiny Gods. We can't do everything God does because we are only a tiny part of Him. But if you put everything in the universe together, you have God. Can you see this?" she gently asked.

I related to her my picture of this man made of light exploding into tiny sparks. She raised her hands over her head and laughed out loud before saying, "We'll go with that for now."

Her laughter permeated the kitchen, and I couldn't help but laugh, too, until I remembered. "Aren't you going to tell me about God's hands?"

She continued, "Our souls are the light of God, or the spark of God. Are you with me?" she asked.

"Yep," nodding my head. I was getting into it now.

"Since we are a small spark of a big God, are we not small Gods?" she asked, leaning her head to one side.

Now here was a grown-up question, and I was going to give it the attention it deserved. I screwed up my face to look as though I was giving the question a long, hard think. But the truth of the matter was, it made perfect sense to me. I put the cookie down, as I wondered about the miracles God made.

She's so pretty when she smiles. "We can create small miracles, young one. When someone is sick, we can help him or her with their housework, or hold their hand. We can plant flowers for their beauty." Her back yard came to mind. "We can watch birds as they hatch out of their eggs, or babies being born. Why, young one, there's even a little miracle in hugging someone who is sad. God creates so many little miracles every day, that we'd be hard-pressed to see all of them. Truth be known, so many people are looking for that big miracle, they miss the little ones."

I understood what she was saying about the miracle of a hug. I always felt the movement of warmth all the way down to the bottoms of my feet when she or Granny embraced me. After that afternoon tea party, I carried that conversation in my heart whenever I passed even a dandelion. I remembered it when my baby sister was crying, and marveled at the little miracle when my hug stopped her tears.

I floated for several days, all the while creating every miracle I could. Sometimes I was impatient in getting people's permission. The little woman said to always get people's permission before doing anything for them. It was hard because I wanted so badly to create a little miracle every single day, every hour. It felt so good to feel good.

About a week later, I went to the flower garden and heard my little woman crying at the kitchen table, with her head on her arms. Worried, I slowly approached her because I didn't want to frighten her. She hadn't heard me, so I did the only thing I knew to do. I gave her the only miracle I had—I hugged her from behind. She patted my hand, but kept crying. I had no idea what was wrong, but my chest ached at the sounds of her sob. Helplessness made me desperate. Not wanting to invade her space, I slowly tiptoed outside. I needed a bigger miracle.

Looking around the garden, I spotted her favorite rose bush in its fenced bed and caught sight of the most perfect bud. The rose bush was what her late husband had bought her for their anniversary. I wanted to surprise her, but the garden shears were in the house. Trying to snap off the bud as I had seen her do, I succeeded only in bending the stem. Tugging at it didn't work. Pulling harder, my hand slipped up the stem. Tears of frustration flowed down my face before it suddenly occurred to me to bite the stem with my teeth, the way I cut sewing thread. It tasted bitter, as it took a lot of chewing before the bud finally came lose in my hand. Never mind the bottom of the stem was bent and badly shredded; triumphantly, I ran toward the house. The blood smear on the rose petal didn't look too good. I walked to the back door and saw the little woman sitting up in the chair, blowing her nose into a handkerchief. Cautiously, I walked up to her and handed her the rose.

She froze. Her face blanched at the sight of my hands. Without saying a word, she jumped out of her chair and went to the kitchen cupboard. She grabbed the peroxide, brought down a bowl, and ran hot water in it. She then went into the bathroom and came out with a washcloth, towel, and cotton balls. Not one word was said. *She's angry with me.* She sat on her kitchen stool, and placed my hands in her lap. She began washing my hands with a gentleness that scared me.

By then, I was feeling the pain. Glancing at my hands, I understood why. There were several lacerations from thorns, one of which was still in my palm. Gently taking out the thorn with tweezers, she touched the spot with a cotton ball soaked with peroxide then sat and stared at me. When I looked into her face, I saw fresh tears falling onto her cheeks. I felt so bad. Looking at the water in the bowl I said, "I'm sorry about the rose, but I didn't want you to be sad. It hurts me to see you crying, and my hug didn't do anything." I put my head in her lap. I had never been stroked before. Her hand seemed to soothe my aching heart. *Please, let me stay here.*

Lifting my head with her fingers on my chin, she looked me in the eye and said, "Child, I was sad because my next-door friend, Ed, passed away last night." She paused only for a moment to run a finger along my cheek, smiling as she inhaled a deep breath before continuing. "I just never thought that before I died, I would be wiping blood off Gods hands."

No one had ever considered me good enough to be a spark of God. It was my turn to cry.

A few days later, I walked into her kitchen and was surprised to find the table set in a formal array. Her fancy cups and teapot were on the table with a small platter full of cookies, and a vase held a rose from her garden. Linen napkins were nestled beside the smaller plates. When I turned to leave, "Where are you going?" she queried with a cheery voice, raising her eyebrows.

"You've got company coming." I pointed to the table.

"She's here." And, with a formal air, she took my hand and walked me the few short steps to my chair and seated me. I became nervous when she pushed my chair closer to the table. "You're my very special friend, and I thought it time we had a special tea." She sat down across from me. "What's the matter, honey?"

"I don't know what to do?" I wanted very much to please her, but I felt out of place. *This doesn't feel good. Something's not right.*

"A friend of mine a long time ago showed me how the high society girls behaved. If you want, I can show you." She didn't wait for a reply. "Your napkin goes on your lap, like so." She took her napkin off the table, gave it a little shake and placed it on her lap. "Now, you try it."

I took the white linen napkin, saw the dirt under my fingernails and hid my hands in my lap. She grabbed my hand. "It's okay, honey. We're not going to worry about that," Then she poured the hot liquid into my prepared cup. My eyes widened when I gulped the hot, sweet liquid. *It's real tea!*

For two hours we giggled over her stories and laughed at poking out our pinkies when we sipped our tea. There were no shoes, grimy feet, worn dress, unkempt hair, and dirty fingernails. Still, I felt like a high society girl sitting up straight, head held high, a napkin in my lap, my pinky out, and properly nibbling at my cookie. The little woman even showed me how to dissolve sugar in my teacup without clanking the sides with my spoon. Oh, how that impressed me. She asked me about school, and I spent the afternoon telling her secrets I had never before told anyone.

In August, I got busy with school and canning season and couldn't see her. One day, I went through her gate and hugged her from behind. A stranger turned around. Looking down at my shocked faced, she had asked if I was Diona. Nodding my head, standing mute. In a gentle voice, she told me that she was Alice's sister, and that Alice had passed away a couple of days earlier.

She talked of how Alice had fondly spoken of me. But I didn't hear much of what she said, as I stood there, stunned by the idea of the little woman being dead. Then a revelation shook me out of my foggy brain. *Alice?* I had never known her name. She was just the little woman to me. Ashamed that I didn't even know her name, I looked to the ground with tears running down my cheeks.

Her sister said, "Wait a minute, Diona, I have something for you." She went into the house and came out with a package. "Alice wanted you to have this."

After placing it on the ground and opening it, I saw the little pretty flowers on the dishes we had used for our teas. I was told to always share my toys and knew my siblings would break them while playing with them. I couldn't allow that. It would be like breaking the little woman. I shook my head and said, "No, thank you," and handed the package back to her. I left her standing there with a gapping mouth. I slowly walked to the gate, opened it, and silently closed it without looking back.

During the next winter, I busied myself caring for my siblings, working in the house, and attending school. In the spring of my eleventh year of age, I went back to the little woman's house; walking the long way around the block and approaching from the opposite direction than I had when I had first gone there. I slowed as I neared her house. Something was different. I stopped and looked into the yard, now bare of the hedge on the other side of the house. The gate was gone. I looked around me, wondering if I had gone in the wrong direction, or if I was on a different block. Thinking that perhaps the yard might look more familiar from the side where I would have entered the garden, I slowly walked around the corner.

Where the special rose bush had stood was a child's swing, looking as though it had rusted in place for years, untouched. Small patches of mud gleamed where the large paving stones used to be. All of the flowers were gone, along with the raised beds. No critters smiled anywhere. There was nothing from before except the house. Even it looked seedy and rundown. Paint was chipping off the windows, and the back door was dirty, with a torn screen.

The shock was too much for my eleven-year-old brain, as I stood there looking at the scene. Had the little woman even existed? She had to! I should have taken the tea set as proof. Where did everything go? My heart tripped when I heard a woman's throaty voice from the doorway. "Can I help you?"

It was enough to jerk me back into reality. "No. No, thank you," I said and quickly turned away. Continuing my walk around the block, I shrugged my shoulders and straightened my back. In the time it took me to get home, I had started to push the little woman out of my head. I had had a wonderful summer last year; even if I had lived it in my imagination.

Things come hard. They go easy.

I will experience more such scenarios in my lifetime where reality touches the other side of the veil and lessons are learned. The little woman stayed in my heart the rest of my life. The things she taught me opened doors I could not have opened without her teachings. She taught me who and what God was and is; and have expanded on the knowledge, as I sometimes teach others. My experience with her has sustained me through hard times. I don't know if she was real or not, but I would like to think so; and the new owners of her home just didn't keep it up.

Long after school opened that fall, there came a Saturday when I wanted to go out and play. As I started out the door, mom stopped me with, "You can't go."

"Why not?" I didn't understand. She had been married for a while, and I thought things would ease up for me.

"Because you're all I have." I fell silent as I slowly closed the front door. She never had to say that again.

I Grew Up

As I grew older, still walking the neighborhoods with bare feet in the summer time, my physical body grew faster than my mentality. Mom would often send me to the small neighborhood mom and pop stores for food items. One of them was owned by a man named Tony. Fairly tall and overweight, I remember him always being behind the meat counter, wearing a bloody apron while banging his meat cleaver on the large square block of wood on large round wooden legs. One day, I had asked for a pound of hamburger, and he motioned me back behind the counter. I naively went as beckoned. He roughly grabbed me, spun me around, pulled me against his body and fondled my breasts. I knew it was wrong, and remembered Moss. Frightened, I pushed his hands away and ran out the side door.

When I got home, mom asked where the hamburger was. I told her what Tony had done. She said nothing, while lighting a cigarette. I realized then how mom seemed to light a cigarette whenever she needed to contemplate something. I never went back to Tony's. Not having anyone to talk to about it, the incident was mentally put on top of my other sexual assaults and shoved down into a dark corner of my memory bank. Still considering myself an ugly duckling, I began to wonder what it was about me that attracted the older men.

It sounds like my childhood was filled with just bad memories or abuse. I was never hugged or told, "I love you," except by Granny. It is hard to miss what you don't get. But there is one good memory of my family that I still carry with me. Dad would sometimes take us for a ride in the large Suburban during the weekends, and one Saturday we went to Strawberry Park in Toledo. I was unpacking the car and putting the food items on the picnic table when mom said, "Diona, why don't you go and play. I can finish this." I stared in her in disbelief. Dad sat at the picnic table, smoking. I didn't respond, but took off like a shot after the other kids towards the playground. I played hard with everyone, not knowing when I would get another play time.

The little woman had always stayed in the back of my head and I would remember our tea parties with our little pinkies stuck out as she related stories to me. I tried to stay cleaner whenever I thought about my brothers and sisters; what would happen to them when I left home, because I was hell-bent on leaving when I was eighteen. There were no fears as I had daily walked the city blocks without meeting anyone. Time stretched into what I began to look upon my life as a void. What I remembered was very little play and a lot of work.

Diona, 5th grade

There were very few surprises in my youth. But in the fifth grade, my English teacher asked me to join him out into the hall. I was very conscious of the looks from my classmates as we walked toward the door. Not knowing if I had done or said something wrong, anxiety filled me as I followed my teacher out into the hall. Standing slightly to the left of the classroom door, away from prying eyes, he said, "Diona, I know you can do better work. And I feel that, as your teacher, I have failed you. So, I am going to give you a D instead of failing you."

My mouth dropped. All I could do was stare at him. I still had no words, as we walked back into the classroom. All the other students had anticipated looks, when I walked to my desk. The rest of the day was a blur. The incident brought to mind that there were honest adults besides the elders. It was the first time anyone had told me that they had confidence in me. I grew that day, and never again did failing work in school. It proved that a few words said at the right time from the right teacher can affect a student for life.

When I was eleven, granny and I were in the basement doing laundry. Whenever I smell bleach or hear water dripping, I remember the conversation we had under the dim light bulb in the dank smelling basement. I ventured in telling her what daddy had done. Granny listened intently while looking at me the whole time. She took a moment before asking, "Have you spoken to your mother about this?"

"Mom won't talk to me about it, Granny. She tells me it was a nightmare, and I know it wasn't." I was almost in tears.

Granny looked me straight in the eye and said, "Child, I cannot speak to you of this." I would learn that this was the code of the south. You did not speak of sex, rape, or incest – especially if it was within the family. Granny had never lied to me. Her looking me straight in the eye told me that she believed me, and that it was not a nightmare. I felt a cold wash come over me, along with the thought that I could not count on my family. Adult maturity laid on me in the moment, and knew I would stand alone from that day forward. Childhood abuse matures children beyond their mental years, often leaving their emotional state scarred, empty, or numbed. The emotions are often busy dealing with the pain of abuse for one to stay immatured. Parts of the brain will grow while other parts stay child-like.

To this day, when a cold wash comes over me, I know I am releasing or letting go of something, and would not go back. In my 50's, I would attend a UYO (Understanding Yourself and Others) weekend conference with 50 participants and twice that many angels. During one of the sessions of that weekend, an instructor requested we lie on the floor and follow his words.

Through meditation, he led us to the bottom of a water source, be it a lake, pond, ocean, wherever the individual was inwardly led.

In an altered state. I swam down to the bottom of the ocean and saw a man sitting on the sandy floor. I knew him to be my first step-father, Moss; but he looked different. It sounds bizarre when I attempt to write about this scene. But while we were down there, dad apologized for what he had done to me. He said it was wrong, and that he was mentally ill. I had been unaware of what his abuse had done to me emotionally and felt lighter when I came out of that meditation. At least someone remembered, and that it was not my fault, nor my imagination.

Gossip

In the summer before my sixth grade, I stayed at a summer camp for two weeks. It was exhilarating to not be in charge of anything, or clean anything. I was also nervous, because I didn't know how to behave in such a social environment. I observed the other kids and the older teenagers who were our counselors. I didn't understand most of the talk the kids whispered when the male and female counselors disappeared at night. As was my practice at the time, if I didn't understand, I just let it go and moved on.

I do remember two events. One was a counselor having to carry me on his back across a creek when someone had mentioned snakes in the river. He was not happy about that and stayed away from me during the rest of the hike. I was an overweight child. As an adult, I would visit the snake area and pet them, if possible, to continually address my fears to overcome them. Also, I think because he stayed away from me, I didn't ask for help. I learned to do things on my own.

The second most profound event was when we sat in a circle with about 35 kids and five counselors. The head counselor whispered to the person to her right. That person repeated what was said to the one to their right; and around the circle the whisper went. When it got back to the counselor, she asked the person to her left what was said. We were all stunned because it was nothing any of us had heard. The counselor went back around the circle to the left and had everyone share what they were told. We found that about every third or fourth person had misheard what they were told.

I never forgot the lesson that day on how gossip is often untrue or things are misunderstood. Sometimes, it is selective hearing or not being able to hear certain spoken words. My husband, Patrick, was a classic example. He nearly got me fired from a job, when he related what he thought he had heard, rather than repeating what was actually said.

Junior High

After auditioning for the Chorus in the sixth grade, the music teacher designated me an alto. I didn't know what an alto was. I just wanted to learn to sing. Chorus was an hour out of regular school hours in the music room where we practiced our voices and different songs. Before the end of the semester, our music instructor had us singing an entire play while on stage behind a transparent curtain. Everyone could see us, but the curtain the appearance of us being invisible. I can remember part of the play, where the actress was supposed to gently use a broom to hit the male actor's back. She swung so hard, the handle broke on his back We, behind the curtain, laughed out loud. We got severely called out for that one. My best memory was singing the play, *Twas the Night Before Christmas*. More than 70 years later, I can still remember the words to that song, though I do forget the names of some of the reindeers. I learned to love music, and found that drums resonated with my being. But I confess that in this modern world, I do not understand nor like Rap music.

By the fall of the seventh grade, I had grown into a quiet, morose young lady who felt like a nonentity. I got tired of the lies my parents told all the time – never understood the purpose. I often wondered if my parents thought me stupid, and felt that honesty wouldn't benefit me. The more they lied, the more honest I became; sometimes to the point of not having any filters when responding to others. That may be the reason I didn't have many filters as an adult. It takes too much energy to remember lies, and you cannot remember them all.

Every morning, I walked the two and a half miles to middle school with the two older girls from across the street. On the days they took the school bus, I walked alone. I did not like the noise on the bus or the kids' childish antics. I experienced enough of that at home. Noises in school caused me to walk a half mile in the rain, if need be, during school lunch hour to a small store for a candy bar or something. After the snow fell, I enjoyed listening to the whispers of tires moving over the packed snow. The earth stilled, as the hush of winter gradually enveloped it. There were times I wished it would envelop me as well, would bury me deep. I don't remember when I fell into the silent person I had become. But I enjoyed going to that place within that didn't ache or long for anything – leaving the world outside.

As a tomboy, I wore jeans instead of dresses. I had equated dresses to femininity. I didn't like the way girls were treated and found that boys had more freedom. I rode my bicycle with four boys, Ron, John, Teddy and Wayne; all living a block away. For about three years, we rode all over the neighborhood and would race our bikes.

We sometimes hung out at one of the boy's homes. One time, three of us were in Teddy's attic. We were talking when, out of the blue, Ron wanted to show me his penis. I was shocked. *What made him think I wanted to see his private part?* Right about that time, I heard someone stomping up the steps. I paled when mom entered the room and gruffly said, "Come on," while pointing to the door. I left with her without saying a word to anyone. How did she know where I was? And the timing.... 40 years later, I told my sister what had happened, and she shared that mom had always protected me. That told me mom had known all along what Moss had done, but lied about it.

Thinking back on it, I knew there were times when I was out with the boys, walking alone to school, or being alone in my room, I was trying to forget the burden of being the oldest and tried to escape it. Blocking out each day's burden was the only way to survive, to emotionally and mentally rest.

During this time, I had started my monthly cycle. While in the bathroom, I saw blood on my panties and hollered out, "Mom." When I showed her my underwear, she left me. I was aghast. *Why would she leave me when I was dying.* She brought back a Kotex pad and tossed it to me, saying, "All women do it. It helps to make babies." That was it – nothing more. It wasn't until a few months later in gym class, while watching a video on female monthly cycles, I learned what the dot meant that the gym teacher put at the end of my name during my month cycle.

I also learned that babies were made only if there was sexual intercourse. Relief filled me at the idea that I was not trying to make a baby every month.

I still had not figured out the elastic belt thing that supposedly held the Kotex in place. All it seemed to do was twist into a knot in my underwear. When the body aches came with each cycle, I readily accepted it as "a woman's lot in life to hurt."

In my adult life, I would learn that the male species of any animal can smell female hormones and know when she is "in heat." A boy, living a couple blocks away, would sometimes visit me. One day, we were talking on the porch steps when, suddenly, he got close to me and put his hands on my breasts and twisted his hands. The act was so sudden, it shocked me. I pushed him away, and he stumbled on the last step and ran off. I didn't mention this to anyone, but did ask mom if we could go shopping for a bra. Over time, I grew to despise them as well. She always seemed surprised at my growth whenever I had asked for something. It was at those times I knew I was not seen.

Diona in the 9th grade

The boys in my tomboy group matured, and went on into ninth grade in high school. Again, I found myself alone and stayed behind, still the naïve adolescent, in junior high school. I still ventured out further into other neighborhoods, sometimes by bike, sometimes on foot. One summer day about eight blocks from our house, I met Linda, a senior in high school. I don't remember how or where had I met her. But I do remember our meeting once or twice a week at her second-floor apartment. She lived with her mother, always with their tiny pet monkey on her shoulders.

Linda was eighteen and I was fourteen, but on some level, I felt we were equals. Being with her, made me realize how much older I felt when with the girls my own age. I often thought them frivolous or silly. I can still remember Linda teaching me the importance of touch as we gently and slowly moved our fingers over each other's forearms. I marveled at the goose bumps and how powerful touch was. Linda graduated, and that was the last I had heard of her. At this point in my life, I began to wonder about those people I encountered. Were they in my life to teach me things? Were we to have such encounters, learn the lessons, then move on? What was the purpose, really?

While in the eighth grade, I signed up for Home Economics, and did the cooking in my group of four students. I had made oatmeal for years; and could not see the difficulty. I was forced to sew a skirt too big for my waist. I didn't tell the teacher I had been sewing at home by that time. I signed up for Wood Shop and discovered it was my calling. Mr. Warner reminded me of a toymaker one would find in a child's storybook. He was kind, grey haired, clean-shaven, patient, and always had a little smile on his round pink face.

When I first walked from the classroom into the woodshop itself, I saw a chisel in the ceiling above the lathe. It was a warning of what happens when you don't stay focused on your work with tools in your hands. I never cared for the lathe, because it was too noisy and too fast for me. The smell of fresh cut wood took me to the forest. While becoming familiar with all of the shop equipment, it was a bliss and a wonder creating something with my hands. The knowledge would one day help me do a lot of my own construction work on buildings and making wooden projects in my own woodshop filled with equipment that men envied.

Learning About the Silence

Sheila was a senior in high school when I was fourteen. That winter, we didn't hang out much except in the evenings on the ice-covered pond, just across the road from her apartment. She had loaned me a pair of ice skates while she taught me to skate on a 70-foot round pond. It was so cold; my nose ran non-stop. I didn't care. What impressed me was the silence in the dark of the night that held no wind, only the sounds of our skates swishing on the ice and our rasping breaths often seen as mists in the frigid air. We rarely talked while skating.

The silence intrigued me, as it penetrated into my soul and awakened a part of my core. I learned to listen to the silence, and realized why I enjoyed my solitude. Indeed, I had sought it out, trying to get away from the role of surrogacy and the noise and the work that went with it. There was a calmness in the silence I had never experienced before, and would spend my life seeking it out in many ways and in many scenarios. The next summer, Sheila graduated, and I never saw her again. Was the pain of getting and letting go a lesson? What exactly was it all for if I was just going to die one day?

In my youth, I would sometimes look at the loss of friendships as something wrong with me; not as a lesson learned. Life eventually taught me that we often meet people who would teach us, or cause us to learn, the many things we need to survive. That relationships are often based on needs. When the needs have been met, the relationships would dissolve. It is rare to have a friend without attached strings or needs. In my adult life, I will have three where there were no strings nor expectations attached to the friendship. Whenever we met, we just picked up where we left off, though several months or several years will have passed. In truth, to me a friend was someone whom you could call at two AM and ask for money to get me out of jail; but I couldn't share why I was there. One acquaintance told me that it would do no good to call, because he would be in jail alongside me.

Growing up as a child, I would often seek the advice of the elders in our neighborhood. In the beginning, they were silent after listening to my adult questions. Often surprised, they would respond by slowly answering to be sure my child-mind understood. When I was in their home, my feet would swing under the chair. I sat with my hot chocolate in my hand, and they with their coffee or tea. I discovered that my mother had often gone to the same people with questions, but the elders never told either of us of our visits. Elders had the grace and wisdom that came from experiences of pain and understanding. I sought out their company because I felt a camaraderie I had never felt with those of my own age. I visited them in my teens as well and found comfort in their wisdom, their patience, their acceptance. It would be more than fifty years before I realized that the elders were just enough "mom and dad" for me as I grew from child to teenager.

My parents did give me some of what I needed to mature. But in adulthood, I became aware of the Universal Duality and how everything has two sides, opposing elements, for the purpose of balance. Pain teaches us compassion and some understanding. But I often struggled with the Duality scale because the pain did not always seem to be in balance with compassion, healing or growth – never mind love.

Eventually, I learned to just let go and allowed the Universe to do its thing; simply because I didn't know what else to do. This involved stepping out of the ego to better see and feel for the sake of growth. The peace and healing that came with the understanding were worth it. Watching others go through their struggles, often helping those while "counseling" them, I unwittingly became my own teacher through observation and philosophical thinking. I also read a lot of self-help books. It was rather serendipitous that the Universal Duality was teaching me as I counseled others. Often came the question, "From where did the wisdom come?"

High School

Arriving on my first day in high school, I was unnerved by gang-related boys in black leather jackets worn by the Fonzie-types hanging out in the streets around the high school building, some leaning on their motorcycles. I quickly walked up the front steps, seeking the security of the old three-story building that held about 1400 students from ninth to twelfth grade. The expansive top step stretched across the entire building front that was filled with lolling, smug jocks in sweaters adorned with the high school letters; flirting with girls in tight skirts, sweaters, nylons, and flats. This was a grown-up world, and felt out of my element. *"Give me children and old people."*

High School was a whole different world, with different kinds of people, different noises. Schedule acclimation was complicated by having to climb three floors of stairs to different classrooms between 10-minute bell rings. I was fascinated by the science room with lab tables. But it seems that science and literature classes were not allowed since college was not in my future – school policy. This added to my feeling like an outcast, a misfit. I spent the next few months getting used to new routines at school and at home. Going to bed late became the norm with homework and practicing shorthand taking up my evenings. I had decided to concentrate on classes for secretarial training, and Gregg shorthand was one of them.

On rare occasions, the teacher in Shorthand Class chose me to dictate in front of the class because I was able to dictate up to 150 words per minute. I had talked fast since I was five. When you get cut off often enough, you learn to get your words out. It would be many, many years later for me discover that rapid speech is often a symptom of PTSD. I loved shorthand and practiced for hours at night, getting lost in shaping the symbols, forming lines and loops, making sure they were the same size as those in the textbook, neat and precise. Shorthand became my friend as I got lost in its world of strange shapes and characters. We understood each other as very few people understood me.

Freshmen were sometimes teased or pushed around; but, for the most part, we were just ignored. I learned right away who the male jocks were by their struts. Female jocks were snobbish and always huddled in groups, giggling and holding their books tight to their chests. That is, until a male jock happened to pass by. Now there was a scenario to watch from behind my hall locker door. Janie sees Johnny strutting toward her, so she drops her book right in front of him. "Hey, Janie, you dropped your book," Johnny would say and make a big show of handing the book back to dewy-eyed Janie. You'd have thought the book had fallen over a cliff, and it had been life-threatening to retrieve it.

"Why thank you, Johnny. You look really nice in your school sweater," she would respond with a sappy smile while batting her eyes—like he'd gone over that cliff just for her. *If she wanted him so badly, why couldn't she just say so?* To me, it seemed like a lot of fuss for a whole lot of nothing. But, then, as a freshman, I was not into boys. You know, just new at letting go of my tomboy ways.

There wasn't time to worry about being popular. I still occasionally walked to school with the three girls across the street. Sally was a year older. Linda was my age. And Susan was younger than I by a couple of years. I mainly walked alone, having discovered that I was too old for most girls my age. I thought them frivolous and too young for me. I had stopped asking Mom and Dad questions because we didn't discuss S-E-X at home. And I was too embarrassed to ask my older friends about making out with boys. I didn't know that children are supposed to be taught life's tools like: saving money; looking for dangerous signs from men who would do them harm; know when to say thank you, or no when a man wants you to do something inappropriate. Though I was not quite sure what was inappropriate. I just instinctively knew what didn't feel right. Social graces were not taught. You cannot teach what you don't know.

My shyness of being naked during public showers in gym class slowly dissipated, and I finally figured out the elastic belt worn during painful monthly rituals. It was actually a handy gadget, once one learned the tricky business of keeping pubic hair from getting caught in the buckle. Surprised looks sometimes appeared on many girls' faces when they sat down and the boys snickered. I mean, how could they know?

At the end of freshman year, when I asked about a poster on the bulletin board, my gym teacher handed me a pamphlet about the Girl's Athletic Association (GAA). When someone gives me a pamphlet, it makes me think folks don't want to talk to me. I almost tossed it back, until I saw the letter M in the school's colors. I read that you received a letter after earning 1,000 points; and every 500 points thereafter was worth a bar. I had seen a few of those letters and bars on school sweaters. It was a show of status and accomplishment. That letter meant you were somebody; and right then, I wanted it. I wanted it badly.

Getting the school letter became the most important goal I had ever set for myself. After joining GAA, I signed up for everything I could: selling doughnuts at the games; handing out flyers at the door; joining the Booster Club – everything. That following summer I was the pitcher on the girls' softball team. It felt great to belong to something and to be appreciated for a job well done. After years of being told that I couldn't do anything because I was stupid, it amazed me that I could do anything I set my mind on. I remembered the scene in the bedroom when I was four, and was told I could do anything I wanted. Before going into the tenth grade, I finally understood.

One afternoon, breathing hard, sweating, feeling the aches and pains of running back and forth on the basketball court for an hour, I felt a sudden euphoria. It was like my feet had lifted off the floor as my body became lighter. I stopped, wondering if something was wrong with me. Within moments, the feeling eased off. It dawned on me from where the euphoria came and pushed myself harder to obtain that "rush." But I never quite reached the level I had that first time. When I again felt the rush, I pushed harder and longer. But it faded too fast. The few times I had reached that "high" addicted me. Whenever I practiced after that, it was more for the high than the game.

By the end of my tenth grade, I had 400 points toward my 1,000-point goal. I continued earning points while in my sophomore year, continuing shorthand at night. No one in the family came to any of my games, nor asked what I was doing; never even wondered about it. I was left alone to do my thing. My days of surrogacy were nearly behind me, while my siblings also grew away from me and did their own thing. So far removed from them in high school, I didn't really recognize them. It was okay. I was leaving home after graduation, and I just plainly didn't care anymore.

Music Room

In my junior year, I found the music room. Music was a love for me after sixth-grade choir. As I walked into the room, I smelled fresh air and heard an oriole singing in the bushes outside the open, eight-foot-tall window. It was singing along with the music Mr. Jones was playing on the grand piano in the middle of the room. I just stood there within the room's vast space and listened. My peripheral vision took in the bleachers against the right wall.

Instruments were lined up against the back wall. To my left was a hallway leading to closed rooms.

The bright singer in the bushes seemed to fill in between the notes Mr. Jones played while fresh air continued wafting through the tall windows. Closing my eyes, the moment became a memory. Mr. Jones banged out the final notes on the piano, rose, and walked toward me. Not a tall man, but one with a soft, gentle presence and a long, angular face with short black hair peppered with a little grey in a Dick Clark hairstyle. He moved with grace, reminding me of what little classical music I had heard. Smiling as he gently grasped my hand in a handshake, he welcomed me to his classroom before offering me a chair. He was soft spoken, but his demeanor drew strong respect.

I had heard that the First Choir performed in burgundy robes at many places and traveled throughout the state in the school bus. I staked my hopes and aspirations on singing alto in that burgundy robe. I asked, "How does someone get into the First and Second Choirs, especially the First Choir?" Gesturing with his outstretched hand, he led me to his grand piano. After singing a chorus of a short childhood song, I knew I had failed the solo miserably, and stood before the graceful man with tears welling up in my eyes. Sitting on his piano bench, he peered at me, and in a tender voice, asked "Can you read music?"

"No, sir," I responded, abashed.

He patted my hand resting on the piano. Getting up, he gestured for me to follow him. We walked down the same hall I had noticed upon entering the Music Room where he showed me the first soundproof room with an upright piano inside. In the open doorway, he said, "You can't try out for First Choir until the end of your junior year. Your grades will have to be C or above. You'll also need to know how to read music and sing a solo in front of the choir while playing an instrument." I turned to walk away. Touching my shoulder, he added, "I can teach you the piano while you learn to read the music. Do you have a piano at home?"

Bowing my head, I answered, "No sir, just eight younger brothers and sisters. I guess they make enough noise." *He had such a gentle smile.*

"I can write a slip for you to get out of study hall, and you can come in here to practice for a little while before and after school."

I thanked him profusely, and was so giddy with excitement, I forgot my books as I raced out the door to my next class. Feeling foolish after reaching my class, I excused myself explaining and went back to the Music Room. The room was empty. Spotting my things on a nearby desk, my heart soared to see the note I would need to excuse me from study hall. Another note read that Mr. Jones expected me to be there thirty minutes early before school, and to stay thirty minutes after school. As I walked home after school, it occurred to me that I hadn't told him my class schedule. I decided he was a mind reader as well a musician. Sleep eluded me that night.

Diona, junior/senior prom

About a month before senior graduation, I attended the junior-senior prom wearing a mauve-colored, chiffon dress mom had bought with dad's permission. The juniors were the escorts and catered to the seniors on that dance night. I don't really remember my escort's name, though I do remember he was good looking.

By the end of my junior year, I had auditioned on the piano playing, "Onward Christian Soldier," and sang in alto voice. It was a song I had learned in my youth when I had attended church in the summer while visiting my aunt and cousins. Looking at all those faces in the bleachers, my peers, I found it curious that I was scared for the first time in my life. All those strange neighborhoods throughout my life were never a worry. Probably because I didn't have enough sense. This day seemed to make up for it. Mr. Jones gently nodded his head while I silently sat at the piano.

Once I hit that first note on the piano, all fears left me. I was no longer stupid or inept. I was doing what I loved, feeling accomplished for the first time. At the end of the recital, everyone applauded, and my heart soared while Mr. Jones grinned from ear-to-ear. I floated out of the music room that day. I had been accepted in the Monroe High School First Choir and would be singing at different functions all over the county and state – with my peers.

Senior Year

In my senior year, I walked into my Homeroom on that first day feeling like I had it all. First Choir; on the verge of finishing up secretarial classes for a career ... then the teacher handed me my course studies for the semester.

Quickly glancing down at it, my mouth dropped. The Vocational Educational Class, where I would finish up on my secretarial skills, was between nine and noon in the Vocational Education Building. I knew first choir was between ten and eleven; but it was not listed there. My stomach felt like it had been sucker-punched.

I walked into the Music Room after school classes and handed Mr. Jones my schedule. He read it. It was a couple moments before he looked up from the paper and motioned for us to sit. He softly told me that often life hands us surprises that seems to take away everything we had worked for. But I needed to remember that everything bad happening to us is a lesson, not a punishment. I had learned an art and was good at it, meaning the piano. I don't remember too much of the rest of the conversation. When he finished, I quietly thanked him. Leaving, I slowly shut the door softly behind me. I did not look back.

I had grown accustomed to things coming hard only to have them easily fly away. I would remember Mr. Jones's comment about bad things being a lesson and not a punishment. What I had to discern was whether or not the negative event was of my own doing. And even then, I had to discern if the lesson was teaching something new, or coming from my own stupidity. To this day, I can still hear the oriole singing and smell the fresh air wafting through the music room. I see the vast space with the grand piano and Mr. Jones sitting on the chair with his hands flowing across the keys. I can also remember seeing the photos in his office of him standing, in formal attire, in front of an orchestra of musicians with his baton poised in the air. He was the first gentleman I had ever met.

I had joined the basketball and volleyball teams, and when my grades suffered, I spoke with the captains of both teams. We were nearly at the end the season. I was told I would be left on both teams, even though I would not play. By senior graduation, both teams had one first place, and I received a medal along with the other team members. I also received my high school letter and nearly had a bar. Mom would not buy the blue sweater for me to show off my red letter. In later years she told me she thought it was a symbol of a gang and didn't want me to join. As if that was not enough, I was not allowed to go on the senior class trip to Greenville Village in Detroit, because she thought it was the Greenwich Village in New York. To my deprivation, she had always assumed things without asking questions. At the same time, I had grown accustomed to doing without and never questioned her.

On the large round mirror over my short dressing table, went the red-letter M that held the pins and medals from the other clubs I had joined. They were the pins from the Library Club, Roller Skating Club and the Basketball and Volleyball first place medals. I later added a submarine pin given to me by a submariner. Mom never attended any of my games, and never asked me about any of the items placed on the mirror. There were times when I wondered why I existed in the family, other than to be a slave to my siblings. Often, there was the question, "Who am I and why am I here."

The roller-skating pin was from the days when Linda Kallenberg, Tom, Shorty and I would go roller skating on Saturday nights. We became close during my junior and senior years of high school. Tom was Linda's boyfriend, and Shorty was mine. He was the shorter of the two brothers, obviously. Their mother would arrange cookouts for us. My one memory that stands out, was having a bonfire on a Saturday night along River Raisin. That was my first experience with making s'mores and learning to love charred marshmallows.

Before graduation, seniors had what was called "Senior Skip Day." It was a day the senior would deliberately skip the whole day; and I was not going to be left out. On that day, I felt brave, and headed out the door between the two morning classes. I was just about to step down that first step, when someone said, "Nice day, isn't it?" Startled, I looked around and saw a male teacher standing idly to my right, lighting a cigarette. I didn't know him, but knew him to be part of the faculty. I responded, "Yes," and waited for him to go in. He just stood there leisurely smoking his cigarette. When the bell rang to go in, he casually dropped his cigarette on the wide cement step, rubbed out it out with his shoe and said, "Shall we go in?" while holding the door for me. So much for skip day.

During the spring, I started dating, if dating is what you would call it. I often just rode in the back of cars and made out with the boy; or just go with a farm boy to a function usually held in a barn. The farm boys were usually more fun. A German boy from high school, named Arnold, came to my house to show me his car. The front seats went back into a reclining position, which is where he put it while I was sitting in it. He startled me when he quickly and lightly kissed me before he up-righted the seat.

In school the next day, I heard he had passed around the gossip that he had "gotten me." I cried and said it was a lie, after someone had to explain what "gotten me" meant. I felt ashamed, though nothing had happened. I often wondered why he chose me, because I briefly knew Arnold. I was not happy with the way some of the kids had looked at me after that, and knew the reason for my sudden popularity. Eventually, the gossip went away. But it made me more cautious of boys; and I despised the jocks all the more. I did attend my senior-junior prom, wearing the same mauve-colored chiffon dress. The shawl was restyled, so it didn't look like the same dress I wore for the junior-senior prom. My date was a farm boy named Frank Kekus.

My senior picture

In June, 1962, I graduated 267th out of 423 seniors. Because I knew we could not afford for me to attend college, I never took the courses for college-bound students. Ergo, because of my mediocre grade, I felt I wasn't going anywhere after high school. And my self-esteem still would not allow my mirror to reflect a pretty girl. The week after graduation, I went to the Air Force office. Failing their test, I went to the Navy office. After passing their entrance test, I was told to lose twenty pounds before going to bootcamp. A month later, I had lost the weight, and took the bus to the federal building in Detroit, Michigan to take the oath.

PART II
Navy

Navy Recruit

On July 6th, 1962, after getting off the bus, I told the cab driver to take me to the Federal Building. Taking a taxi in a strange city made me feel a little full of myself. That is until he drove around the corner from the bus stop and pulled up in front of a large building. It didn't occur to me to just ask for directions at the bus station and walk it. But asking questions was just one of the things I would learn to do in the next couple of years. The whole visit in the Naval office did not last thirty minutes. Between the short physical exam, to raising my right hand to be sworn in, I was inducted into the WAVES (Women Accepted for Voluntary Emergency Service). The women of the Navy came into existence on July, 1944, during WWII, to work in the offices; freeing the men for frontline duty. During the bus ride home, I knew my decision to join the Navy was based on not being able to go to college, and thought the Navy would provide me the necessary education for civilian employment. But I had yet to learn to not have high expectations.

A few days later, the over-night train ride to Bainbridge, Maryland, was my first trip by rail. My meals were brought into my compartment, where I slept in a very comfortable bed. It was novel to me to watch the conductor make my bed by pulling the back rest from the wall and laying it over the seat. The clacking of the train wheels moving on the tracks lulled a very nervous 18-year-old to sleep. I awoke just before dawn. After getting dressed, I put my bed back into the wall, the bed's underside again became the back of my seat. I sat and watched the dark landscape. Every once in a while, a house appeared in vast darkness, and I thought it looked peaceful and warm.

The conductor appeared in the doorway and asked to join me. I was actually thankful for the company, because I was starting to get really nervous. He was very pleasant as he tried to assuage my fears. He related that someone from the base would pick me up, and that I would be their only passenger. He was true to his word when, ten minutes after I sat down at the station, the driver in a Navy car showed up. He said nothing as he grabbed my old, worn suitcase, put it in the car's trunk and opened the door for me to get in.

The ride to the Naval Base took about fifteen minutes to arrive at the "Gate." All entrances to a military bases are called gates – front gate, back gate, etc. A uniformed guard came out of a tiny building and peered into the front seat at the driver, then at me, before waiving us on. While he drove what seemed like a long time, I looked at the many, many long buildings while the driver explained that they were called barracks, inhabited by several thousand men and women. We eventually came to my barracks on the WAVES part of a base. In 1962, Bainbridge was the largest Naval Training Base in the US.

Upon entering the building and stepping onto the quarterdeck (foyer), I was met by the CC (Company Commander). There was no getting acquainted with her. After greeting me, she beckoned me to follow her as we walked up to the second deck (floor). She escorted me into a cubicle containing two bunk beds against one wall to the right, with four lockers lined side-by-side to the left, across the bunks. Four more lockers backed those on the other side, with two sets of bunks against the other wall. All interior walls creating the cubicles were opened about a foot between wall and ceiling. There was very little privacy. Across the gangway (hallway) were identical cubicles. Our cubicle had a very large window looking out the back of the barracks. One looked down and saw the lawn with clothes lines, a narrow road, and the back of the mess hall where men were lolling around the back entrance, smoking. After pointing out my locker, the pointed finger told me to place my suitcase on the bottom bunk. The CC silently walked down the stairs (ladder), out of the barracks and to the mess hall, me following behind.

We passed several buildings and entered the chow hall where we passed other girls eating off metal trays while sitting at many picnic-style tables touching each other. I was instructed on how to go through the chow line without making eye contact with the male personnel serving the food, yet silently make my choices known with hand gestures. The women in civilian clothes at the table spoke very little during the twenty minutes allotted to eat our meal.

That night there were guarded discussions among the new recruits. A trumpet played Taps (lights out) at 2200 (10 PM), across the intercom. Tapes meant we were to be in bed. At this juncture, I would like to share that Taps is not a song, per se. "Taps" originally began as a signal to extinguish lights. Up until the Civil War, the infantry calls for "Extinguish Lights" was the one set down in the Infantry manuals, which had been borrowed from the French. The music for "Taps" was changed by Major General Daniel Adams Butterfield for his brigade in July, 1862."[1] Today, taps is bugled at night around 2200 to honor the fallen military personnel. "Tap's is the refrain part of the song titled "God is Nigh" and we female recruits while lying in bed at night after the lights were out. I didn't know about the male recruits.

---

[1] 24 notes that tap deep emotions the story of taps - VA.gov

Day is done, gone the sun,
From the lake, from the hills, from the sky;
All is well, safely rest, God is nigh.

Fading light, dims the sight,
And a star gems the sky, gleaming bright.
From afar, drawing nigh, falls the night.

Thanks, and praise, for our days,
'Neath the sun, 'neath the stars, neath the sky;
As we go, this we know, God is nigh.

Sun has set, shadows come,
Time has fled, Scouts must go to their beds
Always true to the promise that they made.

While the light fades from sight,
And the stars gleaming rays softly send,
To thy hands we our souls, Lord, commend.

We mustered (lined up) on either side of the gangway when reveille (French for "wake up") was blown at 0500. After morning mess (breakfast), we were marched to another building, where we were given our uniforms. There were one set each of dark blues, dress whites, light summer blues, and two dungarees, along with shoes and other items to complete our wardrobe. We had to pay for any additional items. By 8 AM, we were in the classroom, where we would receive eight weeks of naval training. Having sped through the day, it was again Taps by 2200. I was so homesick in this alien world; I cried after lights went out. Two days later the CC came around and told me that if I didn't stop crying, she would send me home. To be sent home for blubbering like a baby was more shame than I could have borne. I stopped crying.

Diona (Dino) in dungarees in bootcamp

Much to my surprise, I settled into the daily routine of getting up at 0500 reveille, and mustering at 0530 AM. We had thirty minutes to shower, do makeup and hair and get into uniforms after squaring our bunks. We learned to shower before bedtime to save time before morning muster.

The first couple of mornings at reveille would often find me trying to shoulder the not-so-short recruit in the bunk above me when we both got out at the same time.

Our routine was breakfast at 0600; back to the barracks to gather books, and whatever else we needed, and be in class by 0800. If there were three or more recruits walking, we had to march in formation, meaning three abreast, lined up with three behind, etc. This was drilling formation. We often walked just two at a time, but usually got away with leisurely walking with three. Classes were all day until 1700 (5 pm), and consisted of Navy History, Navy Protocol, and learning different ranks of officers and non-commissioned officers; and other subjects I do not remember. Not remembering should tell you something.

Meals were tormenting. The male servers knew we were not supposed to talk to them while getting our food, and teased us unmercifully. After my first laundry was done in the evening, I hung it out on the line in back of our barracks. Before breakfast the next morning, I found one of my underwear missing. When I came back from lunch that same day, I looked out the window and saw one of the cooks holding up my underwear stretched between his two hands. That was the last time I used the outdoor clothesline. Our communal dryer was unusual; it was always constantly hot. You pulled out the narrow door holding long horizontal rods about four feet long. You placed your clothes on the rods and closed the door. A half hour or so later, you removed them, bone dry.

Life lessons often came as surprises. One morning, during mid-watch (midnight to 0400), I heard noises on the second deck. Never having gotten over my fear of the dark, I traveled down the gangway with a flashlight in each hand, until I finally came upon the noises. On the floor on her back was the recruit that should have been in the bottom bunk. In the bottom bunk was another recruit on her stomach running her hands over the one on the floor. "What are you doing?" I naïvely asked. They both glanced up at me, breathing hard, said nothing and went back to what they were doing.

When I went back down to the quarterdeck, my senior watch, an over-thirty reservist, asked if everything was okay. I responded, "Yes. But you know...," and told her what I had witnessed. She immediately got up from her chair, leaving me confused in mine, and went up to the second deck. She come back downstairs a few minutes later, knocked on the CC's door, and entered when prompted. Almost immediately the CC came out, went up to the second deck, and came back down a few minutes later. She and the senior watch disappeared into the CC's quarters again.

A while later, the CC came out and went somewhere while the senior watch came over to me, still sitting. After she sat down next to me, in a soft voice she asked me if I knew what a lesbian was. When I told her no, she explained – in detail. After a few words, my jaw dropped. I thought about that conversation all day. The next morning, I was the first one to hit the deck; lest someone had the idea of joining me in my bed. We never again saw the two recruits I had found, and later learned they had been mustered out (discharged) during the night.

Our Company of forty-five recruits, was unique, ranging from barely five feet to six feet tall; every color and race imaginable; and from eighteen to over thirty years of age. The open, room-sized communal showers and heads (toilets), without doors, provided a means for us to literally drop our inhibitions. In a very short time we shared advice, hair spray, family pictures, clothing, everything intimate family members would share with one another. We had a large lounge area where there was a TV and a Coke machine.

There was one scenario where one of the recruits had not showered for three weeks, and developed a bad body odor. We knew her to be the daughter of an Air Force Officer, but she was still having a hard time fitting in. But that didn't matter, when several women formed a "posse" and physically hauled her off to the showers, fully clothed, and gave her what was called a "GI Shower." Her screams told you they had used a brass brush. Our CC came up the ladder (stairs), and calmly told us what was being done was not regulation. She then turned to leave, looked back to the women in the shower, and said, "Keep it down."

In the Navy, no one passed bootcamp without passing the water survival training. Part of it was swimming the perimeter of an Olympic-size pool between the legs of a pair of wet dungarees (jeans). While standing in the shallow end of the pool, we tied the ends of our dungaree legs, and buttoned them up to the waist. The dungarees were dipped in the water to soak them. We then swung the dungarees over our heads then back to the front of our bodies. We slapped the top of the water – blowing up the jeans – and immediately tightened the waist to keep the air in the jeans. Positioning ourselves between the legs while holding onto the waist with one hand, we used the other hand and our feet and swam/paddled the perimeter of the pool. I had to swim that pool three times because my jeans deflated within two to three feet of the edge. On the third try, my instructor caught my arm and pulled me in. When I think about it, I can still feel that deep exhaustion and deep breaths.

We also had a White Elephant that stood fourteen feet above the deep end of the pool, with a four-foot square platform, and a long diving board. Several times, we had to climb up this structure, walk to the edge of the diving board, and jump off, feet first, straight down. As we touched the pool's very deep bottom, we kicked off and swam up to the surface. Bootcamp taught me to dislike the water and thoroughly detest that White Elephant. Did I share that I am an Aries, a Fire sign?

Learning Movement in an Altered State

Three days after the start of boot camp, I saw a notice on the bulletin board regarding drill team tryouts after evening mess. Applying and after marching to the drill instructor's commands for a few minutes, I passed. I am guessing posture and following commands had a lot to do with it. The drill team, comprised of members from other bootcamp companies, taught me rhythm, teamwork, camaraderie, and the ability to focus every aspect of my body. And to do it with my shoulders in sync with other team members. My face displayed my pride in the mirror every time I put the aglet on the left shoulder of my uniform. This was different from my high school letter that I could not display on a sweater. I belonged to something that was shared with elite others of like mind. Our feet stomping in loud unison, our singing in-sync with body movements, gave me a sense of oneness with others; something I had never before experienced. I truly marveled at the oneness – breathed it, dreamed it, lived for it. I was no longer alone.

The drill team helped me through the eight weeks of constant torture from the male personnel constantly stealing underwear off the clothesline and teasing us with them and studying naval history, which I abhorred. At times, it seemed that bootcamp was going to last forever. There was no place to go in the evenings except to the barracks lounge. As in high school, some of the females constantly huddled, giggled, and shared gossip about everything and everyone.

The drill team was better at marching as a unit than my Company 24. After nearly three weeks of drilling, the Drill Instructor commanded our Company

24 unit to left turn. Executing the turn, we continued marching—right into a wall. None of us had marked time (step in place), and we didn't have enough sense to just stop. Three columns of about 45 females marched into the wall, bunching, crunching, and giggling. So engrossed in our bunched-up marching, we nearly peed ourselves when the instructor loudly blew her whistle.

Not only were we lectured by the Drill Instructor, who had suddenly transformed into one angry wet hen clucking for over an hour, we also marked time the whole time she blew her damnable, shrilling whistle. We lost our Company 24 flag that day, representing our lowest dishonor. This also put us farther behind in obtaining the Achievement and Academic flags, with only five weeks of training left. Demerits were added to our names. Demerits are points assigned for every infraction of rules or regulations. Everyone seemed to know each individual in our company and laughed at us; not only by the male personnel in the mess hall, but by other recruit companies as well. Like all small towns, gossip spreads really fast on a military base.

My dress whites

We matured a little more as we took responsibility and worked at keeping the barracks clean between inspections. We practiced packing our duffle bags, folding everything into thirds or rolling it tight. We tested each other's bunks for tautness – not an easy task to achieve. We held study groups for our classes. I worked off twenty-five demerits during my time in boot camp. The electric buffer and I became intimate while using it three times on the drill hall floor the size of a city block. I also cleaned the tiled floor of some of the heads (bathroom) with a very tiny brush.

During our eight weeks of training, we had a one-day liberty pass when we were bussed to Lancaster, Pennsylvania. The rest of boot camp was spent marching, which I thoroughly enjoyed, and working or studying. What was disappointing was not being able to march in front of President John F. Kennedy during the July, 1962, Waves 20th Anniversary. The Navy recruited several hundred women on a monthly basis, so there were also several other bootcamp companies, along with other drill teams. We had lacked the extra two weeks of full training.

What will forever stay with me is the one time during a silent, close-order drill when our drill team marched in such unison, we entered into a different dimension of time. Having experienced the altered state before, I sensed what was going to happen. I went into my quiet center and allowed. My senses sharpened as I listened to the soft, silent falls of our footsteps; took in the movements of our skirts softly brushing against one another, shoulders touching, no speech. We were one movement, one sound…one breath.

Years later, I would come to know this kind of altered state of mind as being the *Now* state. I would come to intimately know this state as second nature, and could easily slip in and out of it. Going back to the barracks, no one spoke. A few minutes into the lounge area, someone hesitantly asked, "Did you experience anything out there?" Everyone started talking all at once, and we all giggled a shared laugher of understanding with deep camaraderie.

Graduation Ceremony

The day before our graduation we were given back our Company Flag 24, along with the Academic Flag and the Achievement Flag. As we marched in front of Commander Kitchen and the US Secretary of State During graduation the next day, they stood and saluted, as we passed in review. I know it was protocol, but I like to think Commander Kitchen was proud of us. She received her new rank of commander a few days before our graduation. When

I got back to my barracks, I found I had passed my seabag inspection with Outstanding Seabag, but missed Outstanding Wave because of a tiny dent in the knot of my tie. It was okay. I also passed high on the physical, and all marks ranked me as one of the top three in our company. I was proud. Graduation day was a very good day.
July 1962, Naval graduation

Towards the end of bootcamp, we had all been tested for our Naval careers. My typing skills got me the coveted IBM school. All of us had made arrangements to leave base, and I took the bus home.

Liberty to Home

My siblings were waiting for me when I arrived home. My parents, not so much. They greeted me as though I had been gone overnight somewhere. Nothing spectacular happened during my two weeks of liberty other than learning that, John from my tomboy days had joined the Air Force and was home on leave. I went to his house to see him, and his mother was very gracious. Watching him over the next few days, I discovered that he was a mama's boy, and that ended any idea of a romantic connection – though his mother would have us marry. The rest of our tomboy group had gone their separate ways. The girls across the street were either married or had other things going on. I learned that Linda, the middle sister, married her high school sweetheart that she had as a pen pal during the whole time he was in the Air Force.

Visiting the elders who had helped me while growing up, I was surprised by the next-door neighbor, Mr. Merkel. I didn't have much to do with him in my youth. But while I had visited him and his wife, she had gone upstairs for something. He smiled at me while we were in their kitchen, then suddenly reached out to grab me. I was shocked and ran to the other side of the table. I ran around the table one more time before bolting out the back door. I thought him a dirty old man and kept silent about it.

I had visited all of my relatives and friends. Mom took the time to take pictures of me in my uniform, and dad showed me pictures of his time in the Navy during the war. Other than that, my liberty was quite boring, and decided to go back to base a couple days early. I also saw that my hometown no longer had anything to offer me. It actually looked and felt different from when I left. I guessed this was called maturing.

IBM School

The IBM School was on a different part of the base in Bainbridge, MD. The school was six months; half of the day at school and the other half at PAMICONUS (Personal Accountant Machine Installation Continent of United States). It sounds impressive, but mainly we keypunched service personnel transferring onto our base and those transferring out to other bases. Marie, a freckled red-head from Philadelphia, was another keypuncher. We bonded fast. We would go to the EM club to drink and dance. Much to my surprise, I found I could drink a lot and would get a little high, but not really drunk. Being a little high allowed me to feel something other than numb. I would abuse alcohol for another 60 years, but was never considered an alcoholic.

December 1962, during the Cuban Crisis, we came back from a Christmas party and had gone to bed. At 0200, the alarm went off and across the intercom came the order, "All PAMICONUS personnel report to duty stations." It was a true scramble as we jumped out of bed, still full of alcohol, and tried to get dressed; me trying on a pair of pantyhose one size too small. We worked eighteen hours that first shift. We were given eight hours off before working another twelve. We didn't even go back to the barracks, but stayed at the office and slept on cots in another room during frequent breaks for the very reason we were using them. No one talked, very few ate. This was the time the Navy recruiter meant when he said we were the Navy's property to do with as it saw fit. A few days later the crisis was called off, but we didn't see any of the over 3,000 transferred sailors come back.

What I wore in New York City

During IBM school, I would go out with many men. On one date, the sailor was so surprised that I was a virgin, he drove back to base repeating, "I can't believe I met a virgin." A few days later, Frenchie, a marine in OTS (Officer Training School), invited me to spend the weekend with him. I jumped at the chance. I mean, it was New York City! After we arrived, we went to dinner then walked around the city. During our walk in Time Square, another man doffed his hat, and I had asked Frenchie what that meant. He responded, "He's telling me that I am with a beautiful woman." Now, I am telling you. I had never had such a compliment, and I floated. For the first time in my life, I didn't feel like an ugly duckling.

In the Manhattan Hotel room, Frenchie had champagne delivered to the room, and it made me feel so special. Going to bed with him was never questioned. It just seemed the thing to do. When we started the sex, he gently asked me to lift my knees. Embarrassed, I felt like the young naïve girl I appeared. The next morning, I made a comment about the blood on the bed; Frenchie covered the spot with the top sheet, and said it was nothing to worry about. I trusted him. We finished off the champagne with a half glass each.

On the bus ride back to the base, I was happy. To think that sex could make one feel so good. I could not keep my hands off Frenchie. I wanted more. Back at the base, he hugged me and said goodbye. I never saw him again. I learned that it took a whole month's pay for him to take me to New York that

Saturday and Sunday. Years later, I would mentally thank him for helping me to lose my virginity in such an elegant, gentle way.

My incestual experiences as a child caused early symptoms of PTSD (Post Traumatic Stress Disorder). A psychologist, psychiatrist, or other professionals were the ones who would diagnose the disorder. There is no test, per se. The disorder comes from abuse or a trauma so bad you, you have no control over it, such as in a war when you watch your friend die. Sexual abuse lowers the self-esteem and causes one to think themselves unworthy ... of anything. One feels bad about themselves and is in need to feel emotionally good. Sex is an addiction that gives immediate satisfaction and makes one feel good, if even for a few moments.

Men were attracted to me in other ways as well. Some just wanted to talk. I listened. Others wanted to spend time showing me their albums of accomplishments. I oohed and aahed and complimented them. I found I could almost sense what they wanted, on a level I didn't know I had and was slowly awakening to. I suggested to a couple of men that they just call their girlfriends back home, rather than date me. They seemed grateful and did so. I assumed my years as a surrogate to my siblings gave me the air of someone more mature than my age. In some ways, this was true. But in other ways, though I was still learning for myself as I was still the naïve person who had not been given life tools in my youth.

Life tools are: being told what to look for and how to protect yourself, when you are a child and an adult male wants to have inappropriate sex, and the word inappropriate is explained; needing a hug and told you are a good person who has merit; being told you did a good job to instill confidence; being encouraged when things go wrong, that it is okay; being told you are loved and accepted for who and what you are; being taught social manners, what was appropriate and not appropriate. They are tools that allow you to survive, be encouraged, strengthened, give you the confidence for you to grow emotionally and mentally.

During IBM school, I met Mac, a First Classman, who was the supervisor of some of the Seabees who cleaned the buildings. It didn't take long to love Mac because he made me feel good; and marrying him was my escape from the Navy. One night I had sex with Mac's best friend during the rare occasion when I was too drunk to stop my partner. When we arrived at the base, he gave me back my underwear, and I was mortified. The week before my transfer I had learned that I was 2.5 months pregnant and got word back to Mac. I didn't understand why he had become distant, until I learned his friend, Sandy, had told him that we had sex. I was surprised by this, until I realized that Sandy had used me and shared his accomplishment with his "friend." Thinking back over the evening with Sandy, I began to understand more about human behavior and start looking into it rather than at it.

I was good at wiring the IBM machines. But, no matter how much I studied, no matter how well I knew the subject, I could not pass the tests. The class instructor tried to make it easier for me, but to no avail. Ten years later, while in college, I learned that it was the stress of taking a test that blocked my memory. Psychology class taught me that stress releases corticosteroids from the adrenal gland and sends the adrenalin to the pituitary gland. That then sparks other hormones in other parts of the brain and disrupts memory. Taking three deep breaths to relax before a test will stop the corticosteroids, slows the adrenaline, thereby releasing the memories.

I did not pass IBM school and was one of the last to receive my orders for my next duty station. When they came, I was given a choice between Jacksonville, FL or Charleston, SC. Marie was given Charleston, so I chose that base. The Chief didn't like us and tried his best to split us up. I transferred a week before Marie.

I saw Mac on my last day. He said that he knew the baby was not his because he had been sterilized. He also told me that he was married. He loved his wife when he was with her, and loved me when he was with me. It never occurred to me during our time together to ask if he was married. I again wondered if I would always be so easy, naïve and stupid. Stupid is defined as you know better, but you do it anyway. I was surprised that I didn't feel as bad as I should have. I was not aware how much my emotions had numbed. My drinking would increase.

Charleston, SC

Greeted by the watch, I saw that the WAVES quarterdeck (entry area where one salutes) was very spacious with two phone booths on either side of double doors. On the other side of those double doors were the dining room and a large kitchen beyond. When I showed my transfer papers, the watch told me where my room was in the left barracks wing on the second floor. The room had two twin beds, one belonging to a first classman, two dressers and an adjoining bathroom. I went back downstairs to the quarterdeck and spoke with the WAVES officer. I don't remember her name or rank, but do remember my negative attitude towards officers had transferred with me. I was given a tour of the barracks, shown the vending machine room located between the quarterdeck and the right barracks wing. I was told where the mess hall was, how people moved around the base and to report the next day in my dungarees.

A few days after my transfer, I went out on a date with a PO (Petty Officer). I don't remember his name, where we went, nor when I got back to the barracks. I do remember being him giving me a drink and becoming dizzy a few moments later. At that point, the PO pushed me over, and I vaguely remember him pulling down my underwear ... pain ... unconsciousness. I had suppressed that night, but forty years later, the scenario would show its ugly head again through a flashback.

The next day I was bleeding badly and in a lot of pain with no memory of the night before. I had a hard time cleaning the bloody sheets and knew instinctively I was no longer pregnant. I could barely walk and felt very weak, but had attributed it to the monthly cycle that came during the night. I also attributed the severe headache to the cycle as well. It never occurred to me that it was a miscarriage; I was so ignorant of such things.

Janitorial chores in the barracks were done while wearing dungarees, otherwise known as swabby clothes. I still don't remember the other individual who was supposed to help me, but I cleaned and buffed the quarterdeck, checked the dining room, kitchen, and the vending area to be sure they were ship-shape. We never knew when there would be a surprise inspection. Not being able to sit for long periods at a time, I often wandered the halls during my four-hour watch duties, which always seemed to be between midnight and 0400.

During my watches, I would think a lot about where I was in life and how I got there. I knew I had a bad attitude and was not sure how or what had developed it. I began to sense a slow burning anger at my core. I didn't know from where it came either, and didn't know how to put it out. It became my friend as it grew hotter over the years. I don't know what questions to ask, if I don't know the whole issue or scenario. I accepted my naivete, but also knew that I was not as stupid as people or situations tried to make me. I had intelligence; just didn't know how to use it.

Everything in my life was the reason for my abusing alcohol. There was nothing else to replace it. It helped me to feel something other than the emotional pain or anger. During many nights, I drank myself into a high. At some point I became numb to everyday life, and didn't care much for anything. I was a rebel who balked at many things I thought invaded my freedom and left the base whenever I could. One day, the captain came in and asked me to be a watch leader. I refused because I knew it was a way of keeping me on base. I also knew it was because she thought if she made me responsible, I would change. I knew something was wrong. Even Marie noticed my change after she arrived, but neither of us said anything. We hadn't talked much at all since she transferred to the same base.

My very firm figure was 38-24-36. Even had a couple women hit on me. Don't think that didn't confuse me. One night in the EM club, many Canadian Navy sailors came in and took up the rest of the space in the club. While dancing with an American sailor, a Canadian sailor tried to cut in. The American got angry and shoved the Canadian. In a matter of minutes, a fight had spread like wildfire through the club. Double doors in one wall opened up, and a lot of MPs spilled out into the room while swinging their billy clubs.

I was really drunk and was vaguely aware of the American who had slung me over his shoulder and ran out a door. He ran across the street, taking time to take in deep breaths, before climbing the few steps and propping me against the WAVES barracks door. He knocked twice before disappearing into the night. The door opened, and I fell backward into the quarterdeck, looking up at a scowling captain. I never did learn what she was doing on the quarterdeck at that hour in her uniform. Nothing was said the next day. I had heard that the club was pretty much in a mess, and a lot of Canadian and American personnel were put in the brig. Thinking back on it, I felt nothing about the whole affair. I was not even curious who had saved me from the brig. Though I did hear that I was the cause of the fight.

Black Button First Appears

I used to go aboard the USS Triger submarine, just to sit and talk with the men, especially Chief Archibald. The Chief took a paternal interest in me, and we often went to the EM club and sat at a round table for eight. After he, I and two of his crew members sat down, the other four seats were often treated like revolving chairs. Different people sat in them, left, only to have another replace them. We discussed everything from the country, to politics, to sex…. The Chief would also instruct me on things he thought was missing from my education of life. I began looking to him like the father I never had.

During the time I was visiting the sub, I met a sailor whom I had planned to marry. He and I took leave and went to Texas to meet his family. That did not go well. I slept on the couch because they did not have an extra bed. All the while, his mother studied me. We got back to the base a day late because of food poisoning. A couple weeks after coming back to base, I received a "Dear John" letter. There was no clear explanation, but I knew his mother had passed judgement. I never saw him again. It was no surprise when there were no emotions about the breakup. It was just another day. I was written up for being AWOL (Absent Without Leave) and given thirty days restriction.

I had purchased a portable sewing machine on an installment plan, paying six dollars a month. There came a month that I knew I would not have it and asked for a six-dollar loan from my "friends," only to be told no. A couple days before the payment was due, a black WAVES, Mary, approached me with the money. She said, "I hear you need to pay on your sewing machine loan. I know how hard it is to work for a living outside the Navy. Pay me back when you can." To say I was stunned at being approached in such a manner by a stranger is an understatement. I paid Mary back immediately after I got my pay check with an additional dollar, which she refused. I will always remember her gift. I often wonder if this was not a pivotal moment in my life when I would decide to give when I had the chance. It made such a difference on so many levels.

Mary reminded me of the time when, about two am on my watch, a white woman, Bonnie, was drunk when she walked onto the quarterdeck. She noticed a black woman in one of the phone booths, and went over and tried to drag her out of it. The next thing I saw was Bonnie on top of the black woman, who was laying unmoving under Bonnie's pummeling. The black woman had always fascinated me when I watched her: walked with a straight back; shoes shined like mirrors; hair always in place; rarely talked, but did so in a soft voice. I dragged Bonnie off and told her if she came back, I was putting her on report. After she staggered away, I helped the black woman up off the floor and asked, "Why didn't you fight back."

In a soft but firm voice, she responded, "You will never know what we have go through to endure in the white man's world," Slow tears flowed on her cheeks as she walked away. I was left standing alone on the quarterdeck, confused and angry at the same time. Thinking on that scenario reminded me of going into Cunningham's Drug Store when on liberty after bootcamp in 1962 with a black man, Ernie, who had attended high school with me. The waitress refused to wait on him. I tried to protest, but Ernie said not to make a fuss. That he was used to it. Until that moment on the quarterdeck, I was ignorant of how some of the people in the black community felt and had to endure in our world.

When I got off the thirty-day restriction, I went back to the USS Trigger, and was informed women were no longer allowed. I was totally surprised but have the wherewithal to ask for Chief Archibald. He came to the dock and explained that a female sailor, and gave me her name, was caught lying on a table in the galley (kitchen) with her legs spread apart with a line of men waiting to have sex with her. The vision made me ill. I was angry because her stunt prevented me from going back on the submarine. By the time I got back to the barracks, I was seething and sought her out.

I found her in the vending area and confronted her. She turned around with a Coke in her hand and laughed when she saw me. She called me a redskin. The instant, dark anger blinded me and called her a Spic. I do not remember hitting her, but do remember watching her slide down the Coke machine. Blood trailed from her skull where her head had hit the metal opener sticking out of the machine. Someone else called the ambulance, and she spent one night in the hospital.

Afterward, she gave me a wide birth whenever she saw me. I became aware of talk about what had happened, but did not know what was said. I didn't care. My mood became darker when I learned the USS Trigger would never lift the ban on women being onboard the boat. I better understood what that black woman meant about discrimination, after having been spat on for being part Native American.

AWOL

May, June and July of 1963 are lost in my memory, save a few images that would occasionally come through. One image was of my cutting my wrists before passing out in the hall of the second floor in the barracks. Don't remember anything before; but was transported to the hospital, only to be checked out and sent back to my barracks. Another image was of my lying on the ground somewhere in town. Someone must have seen my Navy ID and called the ambulance. I remember hearing someone talking while I was on the table in the ER, but don't remember the words. I don't remember how, but was taken to the psych ward across the street from the medical hospital. My boyfriend, Joe, visited me once and said, "Between us only one of us can be "off." My attitude changed to the point that my imagine in the mirror was no longer recognizable. So many odd occurrences were happening, and I often could not get a sense of why or what was going on.

People in the psych ward didn't talk *to* me or *with* me about much of anything except to talk *at* me with a "report." There is a memory of an incident of the psychiatrist coming in, and after talking to me, turning around to leave, then going berserk. He suddenly lost it and ranted words I could not understand and ran to the door. The locked door was smooth on the room side with no door handle and no hinges. Even the window in the door had very tiny ledges. I don't know how the doctor climbed that door, but climb he did; screaming all the while. By the time the staff came to the door, the doctor was stepping on God knows what, half way up. When it opened, he fell to the floor behind it, and a wrestling match ensued between him and three male orderlies. I did not recognize the laughter that came out of me.

While in the psych ward, I was given several tests, some oral and some written – three supposedly IQ tests. Someone had told me that the brain is very hyper just before a breakdown. I have often been told I was a genius, highly intelligent, over-smart – whatever those mean. I didn't talk much in groups, but did watch people's body languages a lot. Listened to the tone of their voices. I would often listen to what was not being said – along with awareness of eye contacts. I learned a lot about people and somewhat knew someone's personality within a minute. But not recognizing these attributes within myself, and still needing and wanting to be loved for who and what I was, I would often walk into trouble.

Another image always stayed in the shadows of my brain. The image of kneeling on a floor the color of battleship gray, hard and cold. In the image, I am sitting on my heels, naked, with my hands tied behind my back. Three men stood naked in a triangle in close proximity around me. A gun is pointed at me with the man saying, "Do it or I will shoot." The reason for that image never fully materialize and still haunts me to this day. Always did sense that it was in the basement of the officers' quarters during the three months of lost memory. I think I was drugged enough to be able function during the daytime hours.

I don't remember much after my hospital discharge, except people avoiding me like a plague. Marie had never visited me in the hospital, but my "best" friend visit me in my barracks room a couple of times. I didn't care that I rarely saw her – I had numbed nearly all emotions. I did have another image of my stepping off the bus while in town, but don't know why I was there nor remember going back to the base. I do not remember anything of the latter part of June or anything of the month of July. August was vague and so was September. I do remember Marie and I deciding to go AWOL and were going to her aunt's house in Philadelphia where Marie grew up. We'd had enough of the Navy.

I must have mentioned our decision to my roommate, Cassie, because as I was leaving, she informed me that she had called security and told our barracks captain. Marie and I got into a waiting vehicle parked behind the back door and drove off the base before security could catch up with us. We were driven to the highway with our luggages and my wedding dress, if you can believe it. During the two-day trip of hitch-hiking and riding, we rode in a car with two men on their way to Las Vegas who wanted us to act as their wives. We said no, so they parked us close to the Pennsylvania border. I had often wondered why we didn't accept, other than Vegas was in the opposite direction we were traveling.

When we finally made it to Marie's aunt in Philadelphia late in the evening, her demeanor indicated she had not been told of our coming. She was not happy while she showed us the bedroom. During the night, we heard cop cars outside the window, and realized they were called after we had gone to bed. We went out the window with our luggages, leaving my wedding dress behind. Never really understood why I took it. We ran for several blocks then started hitchhiking again, once we reached a major highway. We had no money for a bus ticket to go back to the base. Truthfully, I don't know what possessed us to leave the base in the first place without any money – certainly no common sense.

Travel was still slow when on the third day, a vehicle with two men stopped. When we saw one man in the front seat and a man in the back seat with a cast up to his hip, we felt it was okay to go with them to their apartment. We were exhausted after two nights with no sleep. An L-shaped sofa was offered, each side long enough to accommodate a sleeping person. Marie was smart and kept her clothes on, whereas I, not so smart, stripped down to my slip. In the middle of the night, something woke me out of a dead sleep, and I rolled my eyes around the room. I saw five men casually standing around the L-shaped sofa and sitting on the coffee table. Marie had sat up, and I slipped on my skirt and blouse under the covers then sat up to put on my shoes.

"We want a sex party," one of the men said. Marie didn't say anything, but was looking warily as the men moved closer. I got up and went to my luggage and said, "I don't think so." Being the big mouth, I mentioned in the car about us being AWOL. I wondered if I wasn't hoping someone would have stopped us from leaving our home base. One of them said he was an MP, and that he would not report us being AWOL. When we didn't respond, the MP opened the patio door that led down a steep hill to the four-lane highway and said, "You can go out this way." We left, dragging our luggages, slipping and sliding our way down the hill. It was dawn with little light.

So exhausted when we got to the highway, I sat on my suitcase on the double yellow lines with my cigarette lighter. I scanned a map that I had bought some time when I had my wherewithal to buy one when we were in a store. Suddenly, a set of lights came from behind me that were so bright, I couldn't see anything. I shouted, "Hey, turn those damn things off." Then I looked around and saw two uniforms walking towards me, though I could not see their faces. "Where is your friend?" one of the shadows asked. "I don't know, but I think she may be up that road," I responded, pointing to a road up to the right. I realized then that she had seen them and was trying to escape. I was too bone-tried to care.

Marie wasn't too far up the side street, when we picked her up before being driven to Aberdeen Naval Base in Maryland. In the back seat of the police car, I started laughing for no other reason. I hadn't seen the 4-star Air Force General sitting in the back seat with us, until he seemed to appear out of nowhere. I laughed at everything said or done, often leaning into Marie, who said nothing. All during the ride to Aberdeen, the general pounded his right fist into his left palm.

When we got to the base, we were escorted onto the quarterdeck where Marie was taken to one room, and the general and I were taken to a different room. Just as we walked into it, he turned and angrily snarled, "Women are not only bitches, but their only use is to be fucked to impregnate them and keep them locked up in their homes to clean and cook and tend to their husbands. They don't have the brains to do anything else."

The next thing I remember was seeing him sitting on the floor taking his hand away from his bloody nose. The two large MPs that had magically appeared on either side of the door held me about a foot off the floor, each holding a leg and an arm. The MP in charge, who also appeared out of nowhere, looked at me and asked me if I could see him. When I nodded, he nodded to the two MPs, who then unceremoniously dropped me to the floor. Total exhaustion and physical weakness kept me there. I don't know where the general went, but the supervising MP stooped down next to me and asked, "How long have they been abusing you?"

"I don't know what you're talking about." I couldn't look at him. But his question puzzled me while it rolled around in my head as I sat there in the floor with closed eyes. After a few minutes, he came back with a glass of water and offered a hand to help me up off the floor. He then said in a soft voice that they had called our base, and two different planes were being sent to take us back to South Carolina. *Two planes?* "You are from different divisions," responding to my inquisitive expression. He had taken me to a cot. When I looked up at him, he said, "The guards at the door will protect you until your planes arrive. Are you feeling better?" I nodded yes. Fully clothed, I sat down and gratefully leaned back onto the cot and remembered nothing more. A uniformed woman gently shook me and told me my plane had arrived. I hadn't seen Marie until I arrived at our base.

Captain's Mast

Back at the base, I was escorted to our barracks' captain. She coldly informed me, that I was on total restriction until my Captain's Mast, and that I was to stay in my room when not on duty. A Captain's Mast is more than just a hearing. It is a military court hearing with a WAVES representative as your defense. There was an escort whenever I left my room. The captain's tone told me that she relished the idea of finally being rid of me. The Navy was throwing the book at me. I was threatened with being put in Paris Island prison if I didn't comply with all that I was told. Long ago, I realized, when I was tired, I was numb. When both were felt, it was then I felt truly empty – as I felt in that moment while standing before the captain.

While waiting for my Captain's Mast, I got acquainted with my roommate, Cassie. She was a Third Classman preparing for her wedding. One day, when she had come back from a doctor's office, I had asked her if she was okay. She said she was just getting her hymen cut.

"What is that?" I asked.

It took a few moments for her to get over the shock of my question. She informed me that she was a virgin and explained, "Sometimes during the first intercourse, a woman will hurt when the hymen is broken. The women may sometimes bleed." I knew then that when covering up the blood on the sheet, Frenchie understood more than I did. My cheeks blushed. When she was through explaining, I really felt stupid at may lack of knowledge of the female anatomy. Sensing my mood, Cassie was very gentle, while we talked the afternoon away. We also took turns in cleaning our room and the shared bathroom. We learned a lot about each other during my month of restriction.

It was a couple of weeks when I broke restriction and went to the EM club. The bartender told me that MPs were looking for me, and I left the club. When I got back to the barracks, I had a really flippant attitude. I called the watch, and said I was mustering in. Part of restriction rules was to muster to the person on watch every hour on the hour, except between 2300 and 0700 hour; during which time, I was supposed to be in bed for the night. I also had a couple of beers brought in just before lunch one day, which I drank in 30 minutes in the closet. I was quite surprised, when I got high on those two beers and wondered about being an alcoholic.

Two weeks later, I was calm at the Captain's Mass. My WAVES attorney explained a little of what to expect, but by that time, I just didn't care. She sensed it. The judge took a long time to read the many charges in front of him. He leaned forward and said, "Never in all of my thirty years in the military have I ever heard of any WAVES doing what you have done in just a short time." He was shaking his head and looked very much like President Richard Nixon.

When my mental smile reached my lips, my attorney grabbed my wrist and slightly shook it, telling me to behave. "You are hereby restricted to your quarters for thirty days until you leave the Navy. You are busted down to a Seaman Apprentice (the same rank when I when left boot camp). And you are fined …" I don't remember the amount. I just remember not having much left of my pay. I received a General Discharge under Honorable Conditions. I would learn 55 years later, that it is synonymous to Undesirable.

A week before I left, the barracks Captain came to me and held out her hand. She demanded my insignia – the Navy anchor pin I wore on my hat. I refused, and told her she had no right to ask for it. She told me I was a disgrace to the uniform, and that I had no right to wear it. I may not have gotten along with the officers, but I was proud of my uniform and that pin. She did not get it. Two days of the following week was spent going to all of my stations with an escort. Everyone in authority of my duty stations signed my document that stated I was no longer a part of that office.

Marie did visit me a couple times. She and I had done a lot of foolish things, and one of them was spending the night in a motel with two men. I don't remember having sex with my man, but Marie and her man spent their time in the bathroom. She shared that she was pregnant and it was her ticket out of the Navy. She knew I had changed dramatically since I transferred to Charleston, SC. She knew something had happened to me but didn't know how to talk about it. In fact, we barely talked at all during the month before my discharge. While on restriction, I thought a lot of the three months gone from my memory. They would haunt me for the rest of my life. I thought of my life; what my family would think; why I had changed; who was I; and what happened to the old me. None of my thoughts were shared with anyone.

Before my discharge, I was allowed time off base to look for an apartment. A deposit was put down on a nicely furnished, one-bedroom, basement apartment that was a short bus ride into town. October 10, 1963, I packed my footlocker, and had asked Marie to take it with her – to keep it for me. We made plans for me to visit her in Philadelphia to pick it up. But I think we both knew that was a fantasy thought. We hugged and I hugged a few more people on the quarterdeck. The scowling barracks captain looking on from the sidelines to be sure I did leave. I gave the driver my luggage and climbed into the back of the cab. I did not give the barracks a backward glance. I was done with it all; and good riddance. It would be many years later before remembering that Marie and I had not exchanged addresses. I would regret not keeping the aglet I had earned while on the drill team in bootcamp. I would think of that aglet my whole life, and all that had I learned because of it.

Civilian Life

Within a week, I found a job with an attorney's office. The secretary trained me a week before she left to stay home with her children. It felt nostalgic working in an office again. At the end of the week on Friday, my boss asked to take me home. When we arrived at my apartment, he turned to me, and said his wife did not understand him. Then he asked if I would have a drink with him. I knew the drill and the personality. When I got out of his car, my response was, "I think you need a different kind of secretary than I," and got out of his car. I didn't go back for my paycheck. By the second week, I had a job as a waitress in a dirty diner making $4 a day. When the owner found me cleaning the shelf under the counter, she raised my salary to $8 a day.

At first, I wondered why very few women came into the diner. But understood a couple days later after looking at the type of men who came in. What was irksome was their pinching and patting my butt and making risqué remarks, indicating they wanted me to be "nice" to them. For a day or two, I kept smacking away their outreaching appendages, until the owner took me aside for a talk. She informed me that she expected me to be "nice" to the men. When I told her I wouldn't do that, she informed me I would, or I would not work for her. I took off the apron and went out the door – after I got my $8.

Another two weeks was spent having friends over for a visit, mostly men, because I was lonely. My laundry was done by hand in the bathtub and hung out on the line in the backyard while the landlord looked on with amusement. Not having money for bus fare, I sometimes walked to town. Thinking back on it, I found it curious that I could not remember too much of the scenery, though it did seem to be in a pleasant part of Charleston.

There was an evening when I went to bed drunk, raised my head in the middle of the night and wondered at the howling wind before going back to sleep. When I arose the next morning, I was shocked to see the mess across the street, where a tornado had made a U-shape swipe around our block. The landlord told me they tried to wake me, but thought perhaps I had gone away, when I didn't answer the door.

When in the psych ward, the young psychologist attending me said to contact him when I ran out of the lithium he had prescribed for me. It did seem to help me, so, when I called and told him that I could pick it up, he said he would bring it out and asked for my address. When he came to the door, I was a little confused by the familiarity in the tone of his voice. Without my offering, he walked in, took off his suit coat, placed it on the back of the couch, then sat down before putting his shoes on my coffee table. My back stiffened. "I will give you your pills when you give me a blow-job," he stated with confidence, putting both arms on the back of the couch.

I sweetly said, "Okay," and went into the kitchen. I grabbed a pair of scissors from the drawer and went back into the living room. I picked up a sleeve of his suit coat and cut it off at the elbow with two quick snips. I picked up the cut off end and blew into it until it puffed up. It wasn't until I handed him the sleeve that I saw his shocked face. "There is your blow job. Now, get the Hell of out here." He quickly removed his feet from the coffee table and shot up, grabbing his jacket. "You will get no prescription from me." He banged the door behind him, carrying his coat and shoes. There was no anger within me. Nothing but fatigue. I often wondered why I never got angry when people hurt me. Upset, puzzled, confused, sad, frustrated, irritated … but never angry.

I sat there for the longest time, wondering why men thought me so easy. I was deeply depressed when I got out the wine bottle – my go-to therapy treatment – and drank myself into a stupor. I don't remember how long I sat there. The bottle was empty when I finally got up and went for a walk. I heard the Citadel's clock chime 11 PM when I closed the door to the apartment.

I walked a few blocks, passed the Citadel then to the river. I knew the water would be very deep at the man-made edge with no gradual slope. I walked to the very edge and stood for a long time. The bells had tolled midnight when I had lifted one foot to step into the river when someone said, "Family." I looked around and saw no one. Looking back to the river, I again lifted my foot to step into the cold river and again heard in a louder voice, "Family." Still … no one behind me – nowhere.

I stood there, and images of pain on the faces of my siblings came into my mind at the idea of my death. My siblings looked up to me, and mom had counted on me. Suddenly, knowing what I had done nearly my whole life became untenable. I knew I could not be a slave again, but I couldn't leave them either. I knew what it was like not having someone there when needing support. I turned around and slowly walked to the phone booth on the corner a block away. It was 1 Am. "You will come home, then?" Mom asked in a tired voice.

"Yes," I responded, also in a tired voice. "Once it is wired, I will take the next bus home, then a taxi from the station."

Calling mom for a bus ticket was the final defeat. I had not accomplished a thing during the sixteen months in the Navy and felt a failure at life and of myself. I slept a dreamless dream that night, until a knock at the door woke me early in the morning. Getting out of bed, I had a fatigue that had reached my core; the kind you cannot sleep away. The man wearing all black and a helmet handed me an envelope. I am sure he was curious when I chuckled a thank you. My mind and mood had matched his attire. Opening the envelope, I read that I was to go to the Western Union and pick up my money. Before he left, I did have the good sense to ask directions to the Western Union Office.

Money in my purse and packing my bags, my spirits picked up a little at the idea of seeing everyone at home. I called the bus station for the schedule to Monroe, Michigan, and was told there was a bus leaving early the next morning. I placed my packed bags alongside the door and cleaned the apartment. After dinner time, the landlord banged on my door asking for the rent. I had to ignore him because I just I didn't have it for another month. He had been paid for only one month of stay. The wired money covered only bus fare and taxi. I felt really bad about not giving notice. My landlords were really nice people and deserved better treatment.

The next morning, a friend came with Marie from the base to take me to the station. I reaffirmed my visit with Marie, as she did with me. We hugged, and I climbed onto the bus after the driver placed my two bags into the luggage hold. At the window, I waved at my friends as the bus drove away. I do not remember the bus drive home. Thinking about it, I wonder if the lack of memory of painful events was the conscious mind's way of protecting you.

Home – Not Exactly

The taxi ride from the bus station seemed slow, as I viewed the scenery out the window. The streets seemed dirtier than I remembered, the houses more rundown. No children were played in the streets. When I got out of the cab, my mother was waiting with open arms. It should have felt better, but the feeling of failure did not allow it. What made it worse was the appearance of a couple of my siblings standing alongside mom. I was their surrogate and their failure. My mother informed we were visiting Aunt Helen, my favorite aunt, in about an hour. I was surprised to discover mom was driving, and wondered why she hadn't offered to pick me up at the bus station.

We just walked into Aunt Helen's kitchen when she said, "You have to see this." We all followed her into the living room. On the TV, we saw Jacqueline Kennedy in the back seat of a convertible. It was November 23, 1963; the day President John F. Kennedy was shot and killed. I listened to the women, as they talked of the shock of what had just happened. It was announced that all public transportation would be stopped for three days, and I felt grateful for having taken the bus when I did.

I stayed home for a few days before looking for a job. I went to the phone company every week for about four weeks before I finally asking the man interviewing me if he planned on hiring me. He replied, "I heard about the WAVES. I just wanted to see how reliable you are, besides spreading your legs," and laughed out loud. Walking down the hall away from his office, one could hear him cussing loudly. I had used my very strong legs to push his desk hard against his fingers hanging over the chair's arm rest. Before I got to the street, I knew I would have to take my Navy off my resume. The attitude on signs reading, "No dogs or sailors allowed on beaches," seemed to have reached civilian life.

I applied at a local A & W Root Beer stand. My mother knew the owner from when she worked in a nearby bar he had owned. The job didn't last long after the owner's wife accused me of wanting her husband. Her accusation brought back the Navy memories I thought I had buried in the recesses of my mind. Triangle Restaurant was my next haunt, until I found a job at Ernie's Bowling Alley, Bar and Restaurant. I enjoyed my job of being, cook, waitress, and having the time to talk to the customers. I also enjoyed my employers. It wasn't long, before I enjoyed the coveted job of first waitress with early hours.

My screwed-up sleep patterns returned. I'd go to sleep, wake up with a very active brain, stare at the ceiling, go back to sleep, and wake up tired. A few days later, I feinted by the top of the stairs. When I came to, I behaved like a stranger and didn't know anyone. Scared, mom talked me into going back to bed for a nap. Three hours later, I awoke and was fine. It was my turn to be scared; scared of losing my mind, because I couldn't remember the incident at all. My sister, Linda, was quick to tell me what had happened. If mom had told me, I would not have believed it, since she was still telling her lies. The days melded together as I went to work at the bar/restaurant/bowling alley in a cab, usually driven by the same driver who had taken mom to work. After work, I would often go to another bar where I was offered a ride home. I slept late.

About a year at the bowling alley, I got pregnant. When I told the father, he informed me he was married and said her name. Others had told me she was the town's biggest whore, which didn't say much for me. I filed a paternity suit against him, for which he was jailed overnight. Nearly six months pregnant, dad and I were in the hospital elevator, when I had asked about the accompanying nurse's look when she saw us. "She was your mother's nurse, when she gave birth to Ralph." My brother had been born five months earlier. He was 21 years my junior and my mother's tenth child. She informed me that she would have raised my child as her own as my brother. I didn't respond. I wanted the baby, though I still did not understand why I was "losing it." During this era, you were called a whore if you were pregnant and not married. Mom didn't want me to feel the same stigma she had been given.

Patrick's Senior Picture 1962

I got along with everyone, and the men still admired my firm figure. But I still felt nothing. One night, I had made a bet with my co-worker, that I would go out with the next man that sat on a particular bar stool. It wasn't long before my future husband, Patrick, sat down. Within five minutes, we had a date the next evening on March 1, 1965. After dating for a month, he had picked me up after my 2 AM shift and drove to his house rather than mine. We entered his house, walked up the stairs to a bed where someone was sleeping. I held back, but he pulled on my hand and slapped the sleeping person on the butt and said, "Ma, I want you to meet the woman I am going to marry."

Frances turned over and said, "Bring her tomorrow and let me sleep."

I felt bad and couldn't help but feel there was a reason for introducing me in such a way, like revenge or something. During the next month, I visited his parents in their home as much as I could. I fell in love with his paternal grandmother who had sailed to America while pregnant with my husband's uncle and spoke only Italian. I recognized Patrick's father as a bowler on one of the bowling teams where I worked. We had always gotten along great. His mother, not so much. She was disappointed that I was not a virgin, an Italian, nor a Catholic. I spent a day helping her deliver her newspapers to try to get to know her. Both of us were very guarded, but the day went better than either of us had expected.

After we decided our wedding date in church, Patrick received word that he had been hired by the State of Michigan and would work in Kalamazoo, MI, a two-hour drive away. He was waiting for me to get off work and mentioned about getting married before he left for his new job. While bent over wiping a booth, I kiddingly said, "Sure, I will get a white hat with a veil and use my white waitress uniform…." Standing up from the booth and looking into his face, I saw he was serious.

We didn't tell his family about our elopement plans. We traveled to Kalamazoo for the license, so that it would not appear in the local paper. At 9 PM on a Tuesday evening during a heavy rain storm, we were married by a Justice of the Peace in Monroe, with my parents as witnesses. I tried to back out through the door, but mom pushed me back in saying, "Oh no, you don't." It gave me the impression she was trying to get rid of me.

Francis's best friend lived next door, but could not see through the heavy downpour at who was getting married in the garage. Three months from our first date, on June 1st, 1965, as man and wife, we drove the three hours to the apartment we had chosen a week earlier. During the drive, I was curious and had asked how much money we had. "How much was your pay check?" Patrick asked.

Surprised by the question, I answered, "$84."

"That's how much we have," he responded.

"Where did you get the money to take me to those expensive places, the apartment … all of it?"

He said, "My savings. It's gone now."

Tired, we didn't talk any more until we got to the apartment. It was after midnight, and he had to work the next day. You'd think I would have been happy, but there was no emotion as we undressed and went to bed – both of us feeling drained.

Patrick and Lady, July 27, 1965

There was a wedding shower a week before the church wedding with about 300 attendees. Except for the three from my family, they were all Patrick's relatives and their friends. His family coordinated it, and Francis's friends cooked for it. We had our church wedding on July 27, 1965. Kay, my fellow waitress at the bowling alley, was my maid-of-honor, wearing a dress from another wedding. Patrick's cousin was my bride's made. Patrick's friend was his best-man. My demo wedding dress was $125. My father-in-law paid for the wedding cake from his poker winnings. I paid for my flowers. And the ladies on my in-law side also cooked the dinner for the 350+ guests. Patrick paid for the whiskey and wine. The whole wedding cost us $365, including the gifts I bought for the wedding party. $360 was collected from the wedding shower and the wedding. Patrick ... well he got drunk after drinking a shot with each of the men when they arrived. I told him the next morning, that it would be the last time I would nurse a drunk husband. My wedding dress had red wine spilled on it but stored anyway until it was eventually tossed. Thinking on it, the whole wedding felt like my life: cheap, put together and supported by many strangers.

Patrick didn't want to get married in the Catholic church. We would have had to attend three months of counseling with a bishop and drive down for them every weekend. When he refused, we were given permission by the bishop to marry on the side alter because I was not a Catholic. But when we went back to get the certificate a week later, we learned that the priest had transferred. Our wedding had not been recorded anywhere. The pictures, including those with the priest, were not proof enough for a certificate. Years later, we would assume that the priest had dementia and was transferred to a nursing-home-type facility. Back then, such things were not discussed. Somewhere in the back of mind, I wondered if the whole scenario of the wedding, destroyed dress, his family, etc. were all an omen. My mother-in-law did teach me the social protocol of sending thank-you notes for the wedding gifts. It was one of many social graces not taught to me.

PART III
Married Life

Married and Pregnant

1968 at a family Christmas

Smoking had become a habit while in the Navy. After a couple of years of marriage, I looked in the mirror one day and did not recognize the "bitch" looking back. Anger still smoldered, with no understanding from where it came, or why it sometimes smoldered hot then cooled. I didn't work for a year, during which time my mood got darker. Many nights I did not sleep at all. I took up crocheting, embroidery, any hand skills to pass the time and to occupy my brain during those sleepless nights. I got bored and found a job clerking in an office. I blamed my leaving jobs after a year on my high IQ. I most often would get bored in a very short time. It would be 40 years before I would learn why I left my jobs.

After a year, we moved from our first apartment into a mobile home. Then after several years in the mobile home, we sold it and moved into a luxury apartment. I kept changing jobs, one right after another. It slowly dawned on me, that I didn't like a schedule or being locked up in an office. I was finally happy when I got a job as a keypunch and computer operator at Battle Creek city hall and loved it. After about a year, I became pregnant for the second time and we moved out of the apartment. We bought another mobile home and moved to the country to give our son a space to grow and thrive. Not long after the move, I had abdominal pains at three months pregnancy; and something within me went cold. I felt as though God had again abandoned me and felt less of a woman with a hollowness in my core, knowing I was losing another life. I didn't want my husband called from the ER, because I didn't want him to see my failure. Years later, he told me he had cried that night, because he intuitively knew.

Over the next ten years, the third loss came at four months. Fourth and fifth pregnancies miscarried at three months; and the sixth one at four months. The seventh pregnancy was lost at six months. I was certain that one would take hold, because I had felt life for about a month. No man can ever know the elated feeling a woman has when she feels life in her womb for the first time. We bought a few baby clothes. I was certain it would be a boy, because two other babies showed the signs.

In the ER during my seventh pregnancy, my blood pressure had shot up to 200/140, and I was given an injection to bring it down. It was also supposed to put me out, so the staff had moved to a corner of the room and waited. I heard the doctor say, "If she has another child, she will die." The nurse holding my hand was frantically gesturing to the group that I was still awake.

The injection didn't work. The doctor had to take the baby by pulling on the leg, pushing it back in to get the other leg before pulling the baby out of my body. The nurse kept shouting for me to scream. I had not made a sound during the whole time in ER. I felt no physical pain. I felt nothing, as I my belly went up and down, with the doctor pushing and pulling the dead baby in and out of my body. She laid the purplish-blue body on my belly, and I saw that it was a boy with a lot of dark hair. The doctor used a towel to wrap the baby. I never saw it again. I don't remember being taken to my room.

When I awoke a few hours later, I looked under the blankets and saw something fleshy lying on my belly, held by a set of forceps. A nurse walked in right then and said I would have to go through the motions of giving birth again. Responding to my confused look, she said the afterbirth was still inside and had to come out. Right about then, the doctor walked in. She lifted the blanket and crudely said, "Spread your legs." She pulled on the placenta cord hard enough to pull out the rest of the placenta.

I was then told I would be having a dilation and curettage, otherwise known as a D and C. It didn't matter. I still had not cried out when she pulled the placenta from the walls of my womb. The doctor's demeanor was cold from the time I saw her in ER to taking my baby away. When she left the room, two nurses came in to help clean me up. I learned through snippets of their conversations that my doctor was not liked by the hospital staff. When I later asked about my baby, the nurse said, "It was lost on the way to autopsy."

About forty years later, I would have a flashback of being attacked by three men with sheets. They tried to rape me. They were pulling on my panties, when my thrashing feet landed on the testicles of the one trying to hold my feet. The other two men froze from animal cry that came out of the kicked man. I took the moment to push the sheet off, got off the sand, and ran. This incident was the reason I would wince, whenever I snapped my sheets before hanging them up. It was also the reason I became claustrophobic. I believe this incident was also the reason I never felt anything below my waist, and why I didn't cry out during miscarriages.

Our vacations were not those where we went somewhere and relaxed. We traveled to many places and did as much as we could while there. One year we visited 21 states in two weeks. Pictures were usually taken of state signs as we drove from one state into another. One year, we found ourselves in the Arizona desert in with old western style buildings with false fronts. While Patrick visited a general store, I stayed outside. Leaning against a wooden post of the porch, I was mesmerized by watching a very old wrinkled Indian slowly crossing the street toward me as if on a mission. He wore a leather headband, badly scuffed leather boots, faded jeans and a grey t-shirt with a feather emblem on the front. His long, black hair was tightly braided with a small feather attached to one of the braids.

I stood up straight when he got in front of me. When he stopped, he said, "If you learn to let go, you will be very powerful." Stunned by his words, I turned my head to the store entrance and called out Patrick's name. I turned my head back around, and the Indian was gone. Just like that. I looked up and down the one and only street, with only a few people, and did not see him. I stood there quite rattled and did not know how to tell my husband without sounding like a nut.

In my tenth year of marriage, I had a sterilization procedure called Tubal Ligation. The doctor cut out most of both of the fallopian tubes. It was not enough to lose my babies, but to know that I would never be able to conceive made me feel like the rest of my femininity was gone. I had failed again and was an empty shell of a woman. I laid in the hospital bed wondering what I had done in my life to deserve all that had happened to me, to my body, and my inability to give birth. No doctor had answers. Not at that time, anyway.

The Maternal Instinct

In the ten years of losing my babies, my husband said nothing. I understood his not visiting me nor calling me while I was in the hospital. I never wanted anyone around me when I was ill. Besides, what could he have said or done. I also understood a little of what he was experiencing. Both of us came from large families, and it was expected that we would have a lot of children. I had envisioned myself surrounded by many sons. Both parents came to visit us at one time or another. My mother wanted to be sure I was okay, and my mother-in-law wanted to know if there would be any children. About a year later she visited again, we were eating lunch when she had asked why we always had chili. I told her that I came from a large family and had yet not learned how to cook for two. And Patrick liked my chili. When it occurred to me that she was right about always showing up when I had extra chili, I stopped making it.

My 16-year-old brother-in-law, Ralph, was having issues in school. During one of her visits, Frances asked if we would take him in. While he stayed with us during the first semester of school, he did well with his school work and grades. His attitude had changed from that of a rebel to a loving teen. I knew the reason he had changed was because of our treating him like an adult and loving him. When his mother saw a different son, she wanted him back. A couple of months later, Patrick started getting on me about sending him back. I couldn't argue with the whole family, so I relented. It only took a month for Ralph to revert back to his old self. Frances came to our home again with Ralph in tow and wanted to give him back to us. I said, "He can come back, if we get his monthly check to help pay for his food and clothing and other essentials. And we want full and permanent guardianship."

She responded, "I can't do that. I need a new car."

I looked to Ralph and said, "Now you know where you stand." And he sadly nodded his head. After that, the dynamics between me and my husband's family changed dramatically. Over time, I just stopped visiting them.

Roger - Our First Foster Child

Roger at 9 years old and dog, Rascal

The maternal instinct was still strong in me, so I spoke with Patrick about the idea of adoption and went to the Michigan State Department of Social Services. We had asked for a baby, but I suspected our being in our mid-thirties was against us because we were talked into an older child. We waited for our background checks and finally got our 9-year-old son a few weeks later. During the wait time, we learned that when he was with his family in another state living in a small housing development made for migrant workers, the cops picked up his father for reasons we were never told.

Once Roger entered our house, our lives became a living hell. He had problems with his teacher. He harassed a female classmate in gym to the point of tearing out a wad of her hair. At a parent/teacher conference, I learned that he had used a towel he'd gotten from who-knows-where, tossed it over the classroom clock, and swung back and forth on the clock holding both ends of the towel. I wondered at the idea of the clock not falling off the wall. His teacher was totally beside herself. I took him to a pediatrician who put him on the highest dose of Ritalin, a drug for hyperactive kids. The difference in his personality was like Jekyll and Hyde. He actually laid down in the back seat during some of our long travels and read a book. He was intelligent; but his behavior disorders were something else.

When I went to tell his teacher about the medication, she broke down and cried, and told us how strong we were and commended us. It did not go well with her though. When Roger's personality changed, the school administration, not knowing he was on medication, thought she was able to deal with hyperactive children. They gave her more similar-type children the next spring. She retired a year earlier than she planned when school had let out for the summer break.

We were told the State of Michigan would not pay for his meds, so, during the first year we had Roger, I attended college part-time and worked two part-time jobs to pay for them and his extra expenses. In May, 1975, I received a certificate from the Honors Society for the spring term from Kellogg Community College. That December, I received an Associate degree in Liberal Arts. In May 1976, I received another certificate from the Honors Society for the spring term, along with an Associate degree in Applied Commerce, Executive Secretary.

Roger grew six inches that first summer. We kept a grocery bag in the living room for the clothes he kept outgrowing every week. While I worked or went to school, he stayed with one of his school mates after school until I picked him up. Thinking back on it, it was like my husband and I lived in two different worlds. We rarely talked, because I was busy with schoolwork, homework, cooking, cleaning, whatever – all the while dealing with things inside of me, wondering why things were not working out as I had hoped.

Patrick had been promoted to traveling store manager and was often away. My schedule finally got the best of me. After New Year's, I was hospitalized because nothing would stay on my stomach. During my stay in the hospital, the same doctor who dealt with my pregnancies said I was Passive-Aggressive; meaning I was in denial of what was causing my issues. But no longer having faith in her, I did not believe her.

For several months, things at home kept coming up missing. I would lay something down, and it would disappear and sometimes would reappear a short while later. Finally, one morning I noticed the lipstick I had laid on the dining room table was gone. I couldn't handle it anymore and picked up the phone to call a counselor for myself. I looked on the wall above the phone, expecting to the see the time on the clock. The clock was not there. I slowly placed the phone back on its hook. I knew I had not lost it, because that clock had not moved since I first hung it up. It had become the one secure thing in my life.

Calmly, I walked into Roger's bedroom and methodically went through everything; the dresser, the closet, until I finally found every missing item under his mattress. Still wetting the bed, I found his frozen pajamas between the mobile home outside wall and the bed, leaving a mold mark on the wall. The clock had been dismantled, and the core metal piece holding the dial arms had pierced the mattress, the urine having rusted the clock parts. I was waiting for him when he came home from school.

In his bedroom I confronted him and he denied everything. Rage filled me, and I lost it. Even though it was on carpeting, I backhanded the four-foot-tall dresser and slammed it against the wall. I didn't feel the pain in my hand as. I pulled the mattress up and showed him. He said nothing. My rage was beyond words. Then suddenly, and for the first time in a very long time, I felt the emotional cold bucket of water thrown over me and left the room, shocked at my anger.

After that scene, and for the rest of my life, instead of getting angry, I would go cold, release it, then act calmly. I always found it curious that after reacting to such a situation, there would be no emotions ... nothing. After I dealt with the situation, I would soon forget it and go on. I had asked my husband one day if I got angry when people had hurt me, and he slowly moved his head side to side.

I don't remember the rest of the day or evening, and Roger stayed in his room. The next morning, I kept Roger home from school. With a swollen hand, I dialed the case worker and calmly explained who we were, and that we had one of their children. When the fourth case worker finally came on the phone, I again explained who I was and said, "You will need to come and pick up Roger tomorrow morning. I will have his things ready for him."

"Mrs. Cerelli, we have to make arrangements …."

My voice was calm, but firm. "I said you need to pick him up at 9 AM. If you are not here at that time, I will drop him off." I softly hung up the phone. The next morning, the fifth case worker (Yes, the fifth.) showed up at the door. When she started asking questions, I raised my hand and said, "We have called our many different case workers every time we had an issue. We have learned that we have been lost in the system." During her one-hour visit, the case worker shared that Roger had been in the system only two months before we got him. We were told lies. "So, he had not been taken to the doctor or diagnosed with anything?" I asked. She responded no. I then explained I was in the hospital because I had to work to pay for his meds. She said the state would have paid for the medications. So, they lied about that, too. I had said nothing to Roger after I found the things in his room; not even when I packed his belongings that morning. He moved in sullen silence. Patrick came back home a week later for the court hearing that rescinded the adoption.

Patrick was promoted to clerk for the Gaylord store a few months later and would no longer be a travel clerk. In April, 1976, we moved our mobile home, and I found I could pack a mobile home in just four days. After arriving in Gaylord, I worked a year at a plyboard plant as secretary to the engineer. By this time, I began to feel bad about Roger and called the agency to see how he was doing. Supposedly, they had called and was told he kept everything we I had taught him. He was doing well in school and had lots of friends. That glowing report should have been a red flag.

Patrick had been promoted to store manager in Grayling, a city south of Gaylord. Since I still worked in Gaylord, we bought a house in Frederic – between the two towns. About eight years later, an 18-year-old Roger called collect at four am. In the hour-long phone call, he shared that he had run away from the foster home when was fourteen and joined his biological family in the south. He had refused to be adopted by his foster family. It actually felt good to hear from him. The Michigan state institution had lied to us about everything. He said his girlfriend convinced him to call and ask why I had given him up. I explained how I had nothing more to give him and was afraid of hurting him. That I had released him *because* I loved him. He was doing better and was no longer taking medication. It was the last time I heard from him, but we both felt better after the phone call.

Gil and Other Teens

Still changing jobs, I worked in Otsego County Probate Court in the juvenile section as clerk to the judge, court recorder, and secretary to the Juvenile Officer, Barb. After a couple of weeks working with her, she had asked if I wanted to be a foster parent, which I declined. In a grocery store few days later, I heard this young teen in front of me spout off to someone using extreme foul language. I asked, "What would your mother say about your language?"

He turned around and said, "I wouldn't know what my f----ing mother would say, because she abandoned me last year." I stood mute, feeling like I had been slapped. When I went to work the next day, I explained to Barb what had transpired the night before. She asked me to describe the young man. When I did, she named him, and said he had always been a trouble maker and more than his parents could handle. He had come from school one day and found the door to the house locked. When he looked through one of the windows, he found everything was gone, including his parents.

Realizing I may one day face someone else like him when they were an adult, I told Barb I would be a foster parent. But only if I could have those who were fifteen or older and on a permanent basis. In a very short time, we got Gil, a solemn quiet, sixteen-year-old. But it seemed he wanted nothing to do with us as a family; instead, wanted to spend time with his friend's family. We didn't make many demands on him, thinking we were helping him through a rough period. During his three years of high school, we went through a suicide attempt using an OTC product and alcohol abuse, so we suggested counseling. Part of the counseling was the three of us creating a contract listing what we expected from each other. That worked for a while. He tried controlling us with fake reasons for us to come home when Patrick and I left for weekend get-aways. That worked only once. He still spent a lot of time with his friends.

Gil, the day we adopted him

We went through a lot of emotional trials and traumas with him. Once he graduated from high school, he kept postponing his Navy enlistment. During that summer while in the process of buying a house, I finally realized why he kept postponing. I told him, that we would never move without giving him our address and new contact information. During his first Thanksgiving leave, he had asked us to adopt him. I told him that we had already petitioned the court, and before he went back to his base, his last name was changed to Cerelli.

During one of his leaves, he brought his "fiancé" home with him; never having said anything about her before his arrival. She brought her dog who taught our dog, Buddy, how to escape his pen. The morning of their departure, they laid out their money on the table, or should I say their change. I asked what they were doing, and she replied they were counting their money. I knew they hadn't spent much, if any, and got angry when I realized they had come to our place nearly broke. Gil knew they would get their return gas money from us. I made an elaborate statement about cashing my bond, to which they said nothing. I felt taken for granted, and the cold wash come over me. When I gave them the money, I told them to never do that again and walked outside. There were no hugs, as I watched them drive away.

While in the Navy, Gil would let a couple of months pass before contacting us and asking for money. He had never called to ask how we were. That went on for about two years, until I finally told him I would send him the money, but he had to pay it back. He decided he didn't want it and never asked for money again.

A couple of years after we moved north, I had lost my seventh baby. I was in the hospital for a couple of weeks for the doctor to discern why I had stopped having cycles for nearly a year. My testosterone level caused me to be muscular and very strong. Gradually, over a few years, my body changed from a figure eight to a barrel-type torso; my voice got a little deeper; hair grew on my chin; and I was as strong as my husband. I was placed on Prednisone for seven years to suppress the male hormones. I ended up doing all the work around the house except chopping wood, and mowing the grass. I couldn't swing the axe straight, and snow blowing with the large two-stage snow blower blinded me.

Frederic was a small village between Gaylord and Grayling with about 200 permanent residences. There was a car repair garage; two bars; two gas stations; one with gas, both with convenience stores; and no traffic light. I started gardening in the large space next to the house and found solace in working with Mother Nature again, whom I affectionately referred to as Mother. I had a green thumb and grew my own vegetables.

August 1993

Our only issue were the fleets of snowmobilers – sixty in one group. They would use the railroad tracks across the street that some snowmobilers felt were used too much. Feeling entitled they came to our side of the road where there was very little room between the road and the residences. They thought nothing of tearing up yards, running into signs, or the noise disturbing the elders who slept late. I placed a large boulder under our sign and not many came except those willing to cut into the road to pass it. I did wonder a couple of times what would happen if someone had run into the sign.

Eventually, we would have two teenage foster daughters and learned that the females were more messed up than the males. Other veteran foster parents agreed and said it had been getting worse. Patrick was oblivious when one of them made a pass at him. She was also the one who had all but backed up a truck to steal whatever she could when we moved into our new home. Injuring my back while cleaning out the deep freezer, I could not assist in finishing the move. She did not last long, and the other female foster child was only a weekender. We had six teens in all, not counting Gil, but there was one male teen who stayed a weekend until he was placed in a more permanent home. For years afterwards, I could not remember his name.

When I taught Scratch-cooking in an adult class, everyone had introduced themselves. When I had said my name. One of the students shouted, "You are the one."

"Excuse me."

"I have one of your foster boys, and he continually talks about you; about how you made him feel loved, and made sure his needs were met." I had found my missing boy. We talked after class, and she apologized for the way she shouted in class.

Each of our foster children were told that after school they could walk around the kitchen table to talk about any anger issues before dinner. I was usually in the kitchen cooking where they learned they could talk to me about anything. If talking or walking was not enough, they went out on the wood pile – if they were trusted with an axe. Another rule was that they had to be at the dinner table Monday through Thursday by 5 PM. And lastly, they called if they were out after 10 pm during the week and 11 PM during the weekend. We locked the doors at this time of night. If they could not follow these rules, they did not stay.

David's first Christmas

David was with us for nearly a year until he challenged our rule of not staying out after eleven. When he came back after midnight with his sister, he showed his butt by being mouthy and disrespectful. The next day his belongings were packed and ready when the case worker picked him up. He visited us years later, after he got out of prison. I never knew the reason for his incarceration, or why his wife had divorced him. But he shared that he regretted what he had done and understood why he had to leave. About twenty years later, we learned that he never remarried and became a long-haul truck driver. After buying a house in a different state, his mother and his sister and her family moved in with him. They had all made peace and he was the king of his house. We connected on FaceBook and tried to meet, but it never happened.

Van Sau Nguyen

We were called by another agency to take in a Vietnamese teenager. His name was Van Sau Nguyen. But we convinced him to call himself Van rather than Sau (pronounced sow) to prevent any pig jokes. His story was that his mother converted all of their possessions to gold to allow him to sail to the US. During the trip, his ship was robbed by pirates, and they arrived in port with nothing. Van did not speak English, though I was certain he understood more than he let on. Often, we called an interpreter. David and Van did not get along, and we learned that Van was the problem.

The agency would not take him back for the two weeks we vacationed on Fripp Island, so, we had to put the two boys in the back in the covered truck bed. That did not bode well as the two were constantly at each other. While on the island, we learned that Van did not like dressing up for dinner. He kept running to the beach, creating a lot of lost time looking for him. We had saved for months for that trip, only to have it ruined by Van's behavior.

I knew the agency would give me excuses, so when we got back, I told them that I needed a break from fostering. When Van left to go into another home,

I gave him an envelope containing the bills for his clothes we had bought for him. He was to give the envelope to his case worker, but he gave it to the foster mother instead. The agency was not happy. We received a check after I told them we would not take him back. I learned later that before he came to us, Van had been placed in nearly every foster home the Catholic Agency had. In the end, he ran away to the Vietnamese community in Detroit, Michigan and stayed there.

Patrick

No matter how much I thought life was against me, there would be scenarios that reminded me that we do have blessings. Sometimes my internal energy made me restless and required me to keep moving. Often, Patrick would drive me around, especially at midnight during a full moon. It was a beautiful summer day, and it was our 14th wedding anniversary. I walked out to where Patrick was working on the wood pile. "I want to go for a ride," I said.

He responded, "I just got started here, I would like to work a little longer and finish splitting these logs."

"Where is your sense of adventure?" I was not happy and stood with my hands on my hips.

He stood up and looked at me like I was something strange that had just appeared out of nowhere. He took his handkerchief out of the back pocket of his overalls. Taking his time, he took off the hat I had been wanting to toss into the burn barrel for a couple years. He slowly wiped the inside of his hat brim before placing it back on his head while taking his time to think. I noticed while he put his hands on his hips, his torso shook a little. *Uh, oh, He's upset.*

He stared hard at me and in a firm voice said, "Woman, I entered into an adventure fourteen years ago, and I am still in it."

Having no comment, I turned around and walked back to the house. A couple of hours later, he came in, showered, and dressed. When he came out of the bedroom, he said, "Let's go for a ride." It was times like those that I felt blessed for having a partner who understood me.

Patrick and I joined the Catholic church in Gaylord. After our marriage, I took catechism lessons for about two years to become a Catholic. I could not get past the story of Mary being a virgin before, during and after the birth of

Christ. It took a hip priest to explain it from the church's point of view. We attended church for quite a while, until one day Patrick decided he didn't want to go anymore. After our move to Frederic, I continued but transferred to a church in Grayling, where I eventually became a Eucharist Minister.

When the other lay ministers became aware of my schedule and dependability, they stopped coming. Out of obligation, I did service every Sunday rather than just once or twice a month. After several years, I stopped. I felt bad until Father Bill, with whom I had become good friends, said it was okay, and that he understood. I really liked him. We remained friends even after he left the church, married, and moved away. He and his wife had a daughter, and he lived long enough to see her graduate from high school. He once made a comment on being depressed for many years but had gotten rid of it. I hadn't thought it was possible to just get rid of depression. When I asked him how, he responded, "I got married."

PART IV
Empty Nest

Always Moving

While working for the judge in Gaylord, it was required that all new court employees attend a week-long Basic Law class at Central Michigan University. The course was worth two credits; so, while there, I put in my student application and was accepted into the university without taking the SAT test. I had entered the university through the back door, so to speak. I quit the job in Gaylord and went to a state job as clerk to the Assistant Director of Alpine Center. I did the accounting for Patient Benefit Funds, recorded and transcribed AFL/CIO meetings, and filled in for other jobs around the office when needed.

I lasted there for a year and went to Grayling to another state job as secretary to the director of BUMIR (Bureau of Medicaid Institutional Review) and six CPAs. The office was about block away from Patrick's work place, so we sometimes drove to work together. My boss was a heavy smoker, and I became sensitive to the smoke. The ER treated me several times for migraines with severe sinus infections due to the smoke which forced me to leave after a year. I never became tolerant of tobacco smoke.

Credits from the two associates from Kellogg Community college transferred to CMU. Years later, with just a few credits left to finish my bachelor's degree, I would go back to CMU for a Fiber Arts class. I enjoyed traveling the three hours one way. Fiber Arts was the reason I left college and opened my studio. At the same time, I attended Kirtland Community college for computer classes and received a certificate for Word Processing Specialist. Education was always a given.

A Different Altered State

For our first time canoeing together, my husband and I paddled down the Manistee River after a night of torrential rain. The river was high, running fast, and very, very cold. We never could do much as a team, and this trip was no exception. Rather than using his oar to stop the canoe, he would grab onto a branch wherever he could find one. I nagged him about it, and showed him how to use the oar; but he kept grabbing things. At times he would surprise me by how many fears he had.

We had not been far down the river when he grabbed onto a very large, long, overhanging branch. At the same time, I was back peddling with my oar when things got surreal. With Patrick stopping the canoe and me back peddling, the boat tipped to my right. I slid off the seat hitting the water butt first in a sitting position. The canoe tipped over, and the edge hit the top of my forehead. I sank while still in a sitting position to the bottom of the river. I found it curious that I had no control over the whole thing while it all happened in slow motion.

Sitting on the bottom of the river, looking up to the water's surface, I saw Granny, dead eight years, standing on shore. She stood at a very bright doorway in the dress she had been buried in. I instinctively knew she was there to help me over to the other side. The moment didn't last long. When I opened my eyes again, I realized I was surrounded by water and jumped up from the river floor like a bobber on a fishing line. Patrick was on shore and had to wade the river to help me across when the river threatened to take me with the current. After a of couple steps, my foot got caught in an unseen pile of wood under the water, badly scraping my leg. Neither of us said a word after I got on his side of shore, and we walked back to the boat launch. The owner was not happy about having to retrieve the canoe we left behind. I think it occurred to both of us that we could have drowned in that rushing water.

Though I was soaked, dirty and bloody, I was mad as a wet hen at Patrick for losing his license in the river. I was forced to drive since my purse and license were in the car. On the way home, we stopped off at a local bar that attracted the cops every Saturday night. When I opened the squeaky door, all conversation stopped as I sloshed my way to the bar. My sneakers were still that wet. The music had also stopped playing. I tossed a wet dollar bill on the counter – never did understand why I had thought to put money in my bra – and said, "A pack of Winstons and something to light them." Two cigarette lighters were slid down the counter on either side of me. My hands shook as I opened the pack, took out a cigarette and lit it. Taking a moment to enjoy the inhale, I slid both lighters back to the owners and said, "Thanks," before turning around and sloshing back out the door. When it banged behind me, the music and talk resumed. When I got into the car, Patrick said nothing as I took a few more drags on that well-earned cigarette before turning the car key.

I looked at my wet, dirty yellow shorts and the blood on my yellow sleeveless top. The rear-view mirror showed the bloody gash on my forehead and my matted hair. I understood the silence in the bar. It seemed that every time I wore that yellow outfit, I always got soaked. The next morning, I awoke with a severe headache and went to ER where I was diagnosed with a concussion. I remembered my body lying on the river's bottom and my spirit rose above the river. I saw Patrick looking for his wallet on the other side of the creek. I mentioned this to the doctor and asked why I had not drowned. He said that the combination of the cold water and the shock of being hit on the head could have been the reasons my breathing had stopped. Both could have been what saved my life. My legs were blue when I came out of the water. He did not comment on my spirit rising above the water. I never saw my yellow shorts and top again.

The accident had opened a door to my inner consciousness. Early one morning, Buddy was barking like crazy. I walked out the door to his pen and softly spoke with him. Not being able to see what was upsetting him, I calmed him down before walking back into the house. The sun had not yet risen. Patrick opened the door for me and said in a surprised voice, "I can't believe you walked out there."

"Why wouldn't I? He sounded upset," I retorted as I walked into the house.

"But you're afraid of the dark." He was genuinely astounded.

I stopped moving when what he had said hit me like a slap in the back of my head. My stepfather awakening me in the early hours when I was seven was what made me afraid of the dark. So afraid, I dropped to the floor of our apartment when the lights had gone out while I was ironing. He was right. I looked outside and saw it was still semi-dark with a little moonlight. The clock in the kitchen showed 5 AM. I made coffee in a daze while other thoughts bounced around inside of my head like soft moving lights.

When I started our garden after the accident, I found that things grew fast and healthy if I touched them and talked to them. Even our neighbor noticed this about my garden when she saw me use my finger to make a small, long depression in the soil and scattered the seeds across the indentation. It wasn't long when I started hearing foreign words in the wind as it blew its subtle breath. I regarded the sounds as the wind's unintelligible musings. Everyone could hear things in the wind, right?

Journeying

While visiting my brother-in-law, Michael, at his home in the country on a small parcel of a large farm, I took the notion to walk around the four-mile square. Nearing the end of the last mile, I encountered a dog appropriately named Damien. He bounded out of his house and attacked my ankle. I didn't know what else to do but to keep walking. My past traumas had numbed my body waist down, so I didn't really feel the pain of the onslaught. By the time I got to Michael's house, my ankle was really bleeding and hurting. I looked down and saw a lot of blood and a torn sock. I cleaned the wound and threw out the sock. The surprise was that when we arrived home, I could not go out and hug Buddy. I was afraid of him. That fear lasted about two weeks. I couldn't even feed him. It was insane to think I could not go near my best friend, and he was as confused as I was.

During those two weeks, I had picked up a book titled, "Shamanic Secrets," and thought, "Right." It explained how to go into an altered state called a journey. Meditation is going within and just sitting, until you have a blank mind. A journey is the same thing, but first obtaining power animals before deliberately going to places in the spirit world to gain knowledge to help others. One traveled with power animals for protection against unknown elements. I was fascinated, so, I sat down, crossed my legs, and did as the book instructed. I went to a dark place and got my power animals and started my journey.

The next vision I had was walking with my power animal around that four-mile square at my brother-in-law's home. I was surprised then got scared as we approached the dog that had gnarled my right ankle. In this altered state, my power animal got between me and the dog and said, "You cannot bite this woman. She is a good person." With that, the demonic dog turned around and went back to his house. When I got up from my sitting position, I said aloud, "Now that was interesting," thinking only a few minutes had passed. When I looked at the clock, my mouth dropped to see it had actually been forty minutes.

Later that week, I went to meet Nay Mook Nana, a man who had lived among the Eskimos for five years. His name translates to "Man Who Loves Dogs." When I walked into his house, I bent down and hugged his dog, Taku. Nay Mook Nana said, "Lady, people don't usually hug my dog first." I was just as surprised as he because he was right. I then explained what I had been going through before giving him an extra-long hug. The altered state with my power animal had healed me. When I got home, I hugged Buddy, and we talked a long time with my apologizing to him. With his unconditional love, he sat silently and listened. When I finished explaining, he washed my face. He had forgiven me.

After I learned how to journey, I came across information about Michael Harner's workshops on Shamanism. I don't remember where I got it, but do know it was not on a brochure. I attended the intro and two other weekend workshops. Patrick went with me and stayed in the hotel rooms and read while I attended the workshops. The third class was the last one I had attended. I found I was journeying on my own and doing the same work as in the workshop I was to attend.

A couple years later, I was in a new-age shop looking at crystals when someone behind me said, "Hi." I turned and that was when I met Sharon. We talked for a while, before she invited me to attend a group gathering with six other shamans. They were all degreed professionals: a doctor and his nurse wife; Sharon, a sociologist, and her husband, a Civil Engineer; a psychologist; and a sixth whom I don't remember. The other was me, the odd person out and not considering myself as degreed as the others. No one questioned my being there. It is the way with Shamans to recognize each other without saying anything. That will happen two other times in my life. It was a given that I knew what to do. But during our monthly sessions, new doors in the spirit world opened up for me. Memories of my time with them still stay with me.

During one of my private journeys, I was taken to a teepee on a hilltop with nothing else around it. As my animal and I approached the teepee, an Indian came out. I immediately recognized him as the Indian who had approached me in the Arizona desert many years before. He turned and went back into his teepee; my power animal nosed me through the entrance. I was that hesitant because of not knowing what to expect and still surprised at seeing the Indian. I sat down across the ancient man who introduced himself as He Who Walks with the Wind, whom I learned to call Walks With.

I would meet him from time to time in the spirit world, and he would leave me with enigmatic remarks. Afterwards, I would spend months trying to decipher what he meant. Walks With is the one who gave me the name Spirit Moon. It took me six months to understand the meaning of the name. I assumed he took the name from my ability to help others with their traumas through Spiritual Counseling, which I had been doing since I was 21 years old. He gave me the name, No wha' ich nga, which means One Guides Others Out of Their Darkness. I would slowly integrate the two names for a full name, Lady Spirit Moon Cerelli. Walks With is over 200 years old, and I can still feel him with me.

Yes, I know. Who is going to believe all this? It's okay. By this time in my life, I had reached a point where I may not believe everything, but would not disbelieve either. I would store the information in some place in my brain and wait. I don't remember when this started, but it taught me to pause, to listen and to watch. Eventually, I learned to not "forgive," which puts one in the place of judgement; but to "accept" what was done or said to allow the other to grow or change and me to move on. I also knew that I had the choice of accepting the individual into my personal space or life.

Cerelli's Herb Farm & Store

A 30'x40' garage was built and attached to the old single car garage. The front 24' of the new garage were for two cars. The 15'x16' space on the right in the back half of the garage was left empty. The 15'x16' space to the left was the storage room with a door that opened into the old garage and a door in the back wall that led out to the back of the house. Patrick came home from work one day and saw the three taped places on the cord of the circular saw. We bought me a table saw that began my dream woodshop that filled the open space in the back of the garage. And, goodness, did I amass my tools.

A few months after the new garage construction, I was leafing through a magazine in a doctor's office. I think it ironic that being there for what I knew to be a sinus infection I would find an article in a woman's magazine about Goldenseal Root for healing sinuses. Talk about a synergistic moment. These infections were frequent with a few episodes putting me in the ER for severe migraines. I read through the article to find where to purchase and how to grow the herb.

When I got home, I talked to Patrick about putting in a 10'x10' garden plot in the front yard. Compelled, two weeks later I had a bulldozer remove all the trees and shrubbery from the front yard and scraped the ground down to bare dirt. We were about 50' next to the main highway. I then got a very strong, energetic 16-year-old teenager to help build my 150'x75' fenced-in, raised-bed herb gardens which were named Lilliona Gardens, combing the name

Lillian, my mother, and mine, Diona. After the beds were built, landscape fiber went down on the pathways and crushed stone laid over it.

Do you remember the words I heard through the window at the age of four, "Lady you can do whatever you want?" Those words taught me to be spontaneous and to act on my dreams without hesitation or thought. On the rare occasions when I thought about it, I would hesitate, insecurity would set in, and I'd let the idea go. Everything from that point on became spontaneous and goodness, did I excel.

Organic gardening was my forte, and I wanted something different. So, I created a water-plant bed in semi-shade under the large pine tree. One very long, narrow bed had a knot garden of grey and green artemisias. The other long beds created a maze that held all kinds of perennial and annual herb plants. Every herb had a hand-made painted, wooden plaque with the common and Latin names – all created in my wood shop. My version of pest control was done with companion planting, which I also used for my vegetable garden. I even educated the State Plant Inspector. Never before in my life had I enjoyed creating anything so much as I did the Lilliona gardens that were completed within a month. A few months after the herb farm opened, we held an open house and invited members of the both Chambers of Commerce from Gaylord and Grayling. It was one of those rare days that I took pride in my accomplishments.

Cerelli's Herb Farm and Natural Food Store

WE ARE THE LARGEST HERB FARM IN NORTHERN MICHIGAN

The farm consists of over 13,000 sq. ft. of cultivated gardens with a greenhouse. Over 7,500 sq. ft. of the farm is the Lilliona Gardens with

A picture of the Lilliona Gardens before completion.

Free.

over 200 species of herbs. Public invited to the gardens any time from May to September. Group tours of the farm and gardens must be scheduled a week in advance.

At this point, I would say that I began to understand an unknown quality in my husband. He said nothing while I built my future and to do as I wish with the gardens. He even did what he could to help. We didn't have much in common, but I was learning to look at his weaknesses and grow in my own strengths. We had never talked about this; as though it was a given between us.

Discovering that Latin names had meanings, I hired a high school Latin teacher as a private tutor and learned a year of Latin in just three months. His class would do one chapter a week, when I did five chapters in an hour. He felt he was flying when teaching me, so he slowed me down by insisting I roll the "R" in the words. One could hear an accent after thirty days, and I have not been able to get rid of it forty years later.

The counters, cabinets and the spice rack

I went to converting the old garage into the Herb Store. I built the four 4'x3'x18" cabinets by myself out of plywood, outside on the graveled driveway; and carried them into the store. Two years later, I could not pick them up.

Lady routing out the spice rack shelves

I routed the grooves in the long boards to compartmentalize the 16'x7'x8" spice rack that would hold over 252 bulk spices. The door to the converted classroom was to the left of the spice rack. I built the counter, and the steps that came down from the foyer of the house. It took a while to build a cover over the Michigan basement in the corner. Built out of plywood, it contained two walls for a corner, one with a door, and the top cover. The cooler was placed at the corner, preventing you from actually seeing the door to the crawlspace. I then borrowed $1000 from the bank for the inventory, just to get me started. It was during the time when women were not supposed to be able to borrow money, but I knew the VP, and he approved the loan.

I bought a computer and hid my mother's metal desk behind the cooler. When you opened the front cover, it became the desk top. A little wary in the beginning, I became addicted to my computer once I discovered how much information was available at my fingertips. In later years, my knowledge of the computer and research would serve me well as I traveled internationally and wrote newsletters. The storeroom was cleaned out and used as a classroom. I taught 67 workshops between May and September for a few years before my parents moved in. Eventually, mom's desk went back into her room.

My parents could no longer afford their house after dad retired, and mom's salary was not enough to keep up with the utility expenses. When dad retired on SSA, they moved in, and, for the first time, Mom took over their bank account. Confused when dad took the bedroom, mom told me she had been sleeping on the couch while in their home and had done so for many years before. So, I got a loan from the bank and added a sunroom and her bedroom off our living room. This created an alcove between mom's room and the new garage. I still remember Patrick removing so much snow midway into the winter from the roof into the alcove space, he could walk on the snow mound up to the roof.

Mom stayed in her room a lot, looking out her bay window at a hawk up in a tall oak tree. She had never really had a private space to herself before. Her metal desk was there, along with the floor-to-ceiling book shelf I had built for her. Next to the 3'x 3' closet with a curtain instead of a door, I built her bed with storage space under it. I never understood why it took so long for her to find anything. After her death, we unpacked her room, most of it spilling out into the sunroom. We could not get everything back into the room the same way. She literally knew how to pack.

Behind the house, a bulldozer pushed the dirt from the hill top and pushed it over to the side and leveled a wide space. Large rocks and herbs were planted in the hill side to prevent erosion. We confiscated some of the railroad ties from across the road after the railroad replaced many of the ties. The ties were used to border the bulldozed space that became the actual farm. The space also had the 14'x32' greenhouse and two 4'x8' cold frames. Fall cuttings were taken from herb plants and placed in the cold frames for spring plants in pots and herb gardens. Ten railroad ties created the five steps, 15' wide, going down the bank from the farm to the back of the house. Crab apple bushes were planted on both sides of the five-foot deep steps for a total of ten bushes.

Mom in Lilliona Gardens

Mom helped with the business, eventually taking over the greenhouse and the gardens. My green thumb had come from her. She loved working in the greenhouse, though I was not comfortable with her sharing that she did so while naked from the waist up. She could still surprise me. That left me with the books, lectures, and tours of the gardens.

During one of the tours in the garden, some of the kids would point to me and simply say, "Lady." Curious, I had asked an eight-year-old why she called me that, and she told me that it was because I looked like Lady.

"And what does Lady look like?" I asked, amused.

"Lady is an angel with white hair. Don't you know that?" My ignorance surprised her. She had not been the only one who told me that, and it started me thinking. My family called me Diona, and the hair on the back of my neck would stand up because of the negative issues with them. I never really cared for my first name Emma. Within a few months, I went to court and changed my name to Lady Diona Cerelli. When I had told mom about the name change, she was okay with it. Native Americans would often name their children according to the child's personality. When they reached the age of rite-of-passage, they may change their name again. As people grow and change, their personalities often change. Names should reflect that change. I am very comfortable with mine.

Working from eight am to eleven PM from baking bread to packing the bulk spice racks, bulk beans, flour, etc. and selling it all, I had no time for anything else. Within a couple of years, we built a new free-standing building for just the spices and gifts. The old store had then been transformed into a classroom with a large 8'x5' table in the center of the room. As many as 67-80 classes a year were taught in that room: potpourri to herbology to basketry to walks across the road along the highway to pick flowers for living wreaths. Wreaths, made from aromatic herbs for doorways during canning season, were created to keep out flying pests. The large table in the new classroom had also sat 26 people during a Christmas dinner. That was the one and only dinner of such gatherings.

During all of this teaching, I also lectured. My proudest was being asked to teach a potpourri class for the wives of directors of major telephone companies from each state across the USA. The annual conference was held at the five-star Grand Hotel on Mackinaw Island, Michigan. The president of the women's club booked a potpourri class of thirty participants. I had taken enough ingredients for each to make the same potpourri recipe. When the class was nearly done, one of the students asked if I would read the potpourris. Surprised, I had asked how she knew of my abilities, and she shared that she lived near me and was aware of me and my business. I took the time to read the thirty potpourris. It was during this class that I learned not everyone measures the same amount of each ingredient, so no two readings were the same – yet all were accurate. In truth, the accuracy of my skills made me a little nervous, and I began to wonder from where the information was actually coming.

There came a day when I got it into my head to start fast-walking five miles a day, and eventually worked up to do it in an hour and fifteen minutes while Mom watched the store. During these walks, I became aware of things often seen, but not really thought of. I watched a dead deer on the side of the road disappear a little each day. Insects and tiny mice ate on it until it disappeared altogether, and the fur blew up and away in the wind. As each day passed, I watched the flowers in the fields rise up, bloom and die before fading away into the soil.

One day, when I got to the end of the first half of the walk, I stopped only for a moment to turn around, when my consciousness enveloped everything around me. My essence seemed to actually leave my body and became a part of everything. It was like the first time during a high school basketball and learned it is called a runner's high. But in this instance, it was far more. This was the spiritual realm I would live in for the rest of my life. I had found my silence again. I understood it more, as I explored it over time while it became a very good friend. I took time to do things for myself and stayed in my bedroom rocking, meditating, crocheting … being by myself. For the rest of my life, I would take the needed time to heal the little facets of myself, adapt to the changes and grow in and from wisdom.

Two Deaths

The herb business stayed open for a total of seven years. Dad passed away about four years after he and mom moved in. The Christmas before, I was so upset with his lies and always complaining while sitting in his kitchen chair smoking up my house. Our parents had always been the first to unwrap the gifts before the rest of us opened ours. But after mom opened hers, I told everyone to open theirs – leaving dad out. In March, he ran out of money and went three days without alcohol. June, we thought he was urinating on the kitchen floor when we heard the sloshing of water when tapping his foot. A day later, he came out of the bathroom saying he could not urinate; so, my mother and brother took him to the hospital. Those two signs were the only indicators of his being ill. He had continued his smoking, though he was quieter about his complaints. We learned he had stopped his medication in January. I sometimes wondered if my treating him the way I did at Christmas was what changed his demeanor.

Only after I shared with the nurse that he was an alcoholic did we learn that he had suffered from DTs (delirium tremens), that his body was shutting down. Two days later, he raised up from his hospital bed at midnight, pulled out the two needles from his arms, laid back down and died. He was cremated without a funeral service. Who would we have invited? No one had ever visited him. We learned that not many people talked with him at the bar he frequented on a daily basis. Not allowing him to open his gifts after mom did, a form of honoring him as a parent, stayed with me a long time after his death. It was one of my few regrets in life.

Friday morning, April, 1989, mom was losing her ability to walk, so we took her to the doctor. When it came to protecting her, I learned how much of a bitch I could be. The doctor ordered x-rays of her lungs. When I called about the x-rays the next day, I stubbornly stayed on the phone until the doctor came on. He was not happy, but told me of her cancer diagnosis and that his office had contacted the Oncologist in Petoskey Hospital. We arrived at 4:45 PM, just as the radiologist was leaving. The surgeon was also stopped from leaving for Mom's needed spine surgery at 9 PM. If her surgery had not been done when it was, she would have lost control of her bladder and bowels before Monday. The Oncologist told us that x-rays of the tumor in her lung displayed the Oat-Cell Cancer was enveloped by another type of cancer. They did not know the type because the biopsy did not get any of the outside tumor. When I first heard this, I had told the oncologist that mom had five tumors. She did not respond. So far, they had found two kinds of tumors.

We closed the store and gardens and spent the next seven months traveling over 25,000 miles for mom's chemo and hospital visits. While in her wheel chair, she wore the clam shell that allowed her to sit. It was taken off at night. The burden of my mother dying and choosing to close the store was almost too much. I just didn't know it until one day at 8 AM, I had told everyone I was going to the grocery store – a twenty-minute drive. At 11 AM, I called home and said, "I don't know where I am, but I will turn around and drive back." I don't remember who answered the phone, but I never gave them a chance to respond. I just hung up. To this day, all I remember is driving past the store and onto the penetrator to the expressway going south. I still don't remember where I was or how I got there, but do remember asking a State Trooper for directions back to the expressway. I got home around 3 PM. The next morning, I announced I was going to the store to get the forgotten groceries. After the long silence and worried stares, I had to reassure everyone that I'd be back.

I still worked a few occasional hours in a flower shop to keep grounded. On my way home one day, I saw a dead hawk on the side of the road and instinctually stopped the vehicle. I got out to look at it, and knew it to be the hawk mom watched outside her large bay window. It sat up in the tree, while they watched each other for many hours. Cherokee blood running through our veins, I knew the dead hawk was a message. I gently placed the bird in a box I had in the trunk of the car and took it home to mom. I reverently took the box into the kitchen and showed it to her. She leaned over in her wheelchair and petted it while a tear run down her cheek. Looking up at me, we both knew.

The following Tuesday, mom related to me how there were transistors in pineapple and demonstrated how to eat the pineapple without being electrocuted. I listened with a gaped mouth but said nothing. When she finished, I calmly talked her into going down for a nap then rushed to the phone and called the Oncologist. Wednesday, mom had a spinal tap. Thursday, the doctor called in the morning and said that the spinal tap showed three inoperable brain tumors. That made five in all. It seemed to take a long time for me to hang up the landline. The cancer that had encased the tumor in her lung was the one that had created the three tumors in her brain.

By the time I had picked her up on Friday, the house was thoroughly cleaned; the hospital bed was waiting in the middle of her room; and hospice had been contacted. When she was settled into the front seat and buckled up, mom looked to me and asked when she was going back to the hospital. I thought for a moment and said, "Mom, you will never have to come back here again." She looked at me for a few moments then said, "Okay," and leaned her head back against the seat's headrest and napped on the way home.

I had called my siblings and mom's best friend on Thursday, and said there would be a party on Saturday and Sunday. I found it curious that all the "bad" people came on Saturday, and the "good" people came on Sunday. After everyone left Sunday evening, I placed a cot in the Sun room, next to mom's door. My brothers were in the kitchen talking when I told them to let me know if mom awakened. I knew mom was in pain and kept her knocked out with the morphine injections, except when the visitors came. You can't kill a dead person, right? I had been awake 72 hours and was looking forward to a good sleep. Five hours later, something woke me out of a dead-man's sleep.

I immediately got out of my cot when I saw mom's waving arms. I knew her to be in pain. Looking down at her, I saw her one eye, and knew she'd had a stroke. Something within me started to burn. I verbally soothed her as I gave her an injection, making sure she was out. Then, I slowly walked into the kitchen, trying to control my hot core. I told 'them' they had forgotten to check on mom. I informed them of what I had found, then railed into them for their incompetency. That it was their mother; how could they ignore her. I banged the front door after kicking them out. I never thought I was capable of hate, but I hated them. In that moment, I realized I hated the whole world.

My sister, Linda, had left on Sunday. Her husband brought her back on Monday with her twin, Jeri. They were considered the black sheep of the family. Yet, they, of all of my siblings, were the ones who helped me with mom. The hospice nurse came often and didn't really say much about my giving mom the extra morphine. We three sat with mom and played the Elvis Presley music she loved so much. My husband stayed out of the way as much as he could, while still offering a great deal of support. My brothers never came back. Mom passed on Tuesday.

During one of Bonnie's rare visits with me while mom was in the hospital for chemo, I had told her I was not the administrator of mom's Will. I never saw her again. She was good at spreading lies, and was the sister to whom I referred to as the queen witch of Hamlet's three witches. The day after mom died, I received a letter from the queen witch. I will confess that the letter she had sent a letter two years earlier had hurt me; and when mom caught me crying, I shared it with her. She was not happy. This second letter was postmarked an hour after mom's death. Bonnie wrote that during the years mom lived with us, she and my siblings sat around the campfires devising ways to sue me for taking mom's belongings. She also called my brothers alcoholics. It was not a nice letter.

After reading the letter, the familiar cold wash came over me. There were no emotions as I picked up the phone, called each sibling and read the letter to each of them. I then asked each the same question: "Did you, indeed, sit around all those campfires and talk about how you would sue me, as it says in the letter?" My brothers responded yes. Penny and Suzette, the other two witches, responded yes, but also apologized for the letter. My oldest and youngest brothers were not around at the time and were never really invited to anything. The oldest brother, Bobbie, was the mean alcoholic, and mom abandoned the youngest when she moved in with us. He was very abusive toward her. My calmness after each and every call almost alarmed me and had, unknowingly, caused me to make a decision.

Mom and I were the intuits in our family. My brother, Michael, mom's executor, came back from the funeral home, and said he needed another $800 to pay for mom's cremation bill. After much discussion, no one had it. To get his mind off things, I suggested he go in and clean out mom's desk. He came out about ten minutes later with a dumb-founded expression on his face, holding an envelope. We all saw the contents of twenty-dollar bills totaling $800.

Mom was proud of her Native American heritage. Indians have a tradition of giving away possessions of a deceased family member for the deceased to have a new life. The idea can also be used by the living to give away contents of your old life to make room for a different life. If you were meant to have any of the items back, it would come again in the new life. I have done this letting go twice in my lifetime. There is a sense of freedom and freshness in giving away the old and waiting for the new. We talked about when to have mom's give-away and made plans to do it in a month's time. And there was no service for mom. She also, had never received visitors, except once from her best friend.

A month later, we all sat in my living room where my siblings learned that I had not taken all of my parents' possessions, after all. They never said a word, nor did they look at me. Penny could not stay the night when we said we would put mom's ashes in the river the next day. She did, however, state she wished she had hired a truck to spend the night and take back what she was given. Suzette helped her with them. I asked about the extra pile of items laying on the floor between them, and was told it was for Bonnie. I reminded Michael about the letter and how Bonnie never shared in any of mom's health issues, but would hurt her in her letters. Michael then took the items and dispersed them among the siblings who were present. I had already taken what few items I wanted before everyone came.

Still having the cold wash in my core, it didn't matter to me that no one stayed after the give-away to spread our parents' ashes in the nearby creek. It was just me, Patrick, my brother Michael, and the twins who had helped care for mom in the end. Michael called a few days later and said Penny wanted my phone number. I responded, "Michael, you are not to give out any information about me or my family to any of my siblings without my permission. Tomorrow doesn't look good, nor does next week." I visited my brothers, Davy and Michael, many years later, but that was the first and last time I spoke to my siblings, except for the twins. Then only one twin remained, Linda.

In writing this memoir, it occurred to me why I coldly made the decision to not have anything more to do with my siblings. I verified with my sister, Linda, that my whole youth and teen years were devoted to caring for 'them' and walking the neighborhood to get away from the responsibilities. At no time, did I do anything to harm my siblings nor said anything to degrade or demean them. Even after my marriage, I did what I could, even spending a week making my brother's multi-layered wedding cake with a fountain. To have them treat me the way they did behind my back was too much.

Because I could not afford to hire the two employees to take mom's place, the gardens and store were never reopened. And my mourning heart had lost interest. Six months after her passing, at 2 AM, I heard mom outside our bedroom door calling my name, "Diona." Her voice was as clear as if she were standing next to me. I opened our bedroom door, and two surprises slapped my brain. One, mom was not there in her wheelchair. And two, we were still closing our bedroom door, even though Patrick and I were the only ones in the house. I grieved mom for over a year.

Another great disappointment was Becca, whom I had met ten years before through a mutual friend. We met frequently and did a lot of things together. After her divorce from her first husband, she willingly gave over custody of her only child to her husband. Never understood this until I learned more about her personality. Becca was the reason I had gone to Central Michigan University for my Fiber Art Class. She was trying to complete her master's in Library Science and didn't want to attend the first semester alone.

She had also taken a sculpting class. Everyone complimented her on her art piece which she said "was in the clay." Leisurely looking through the art books in the campus library, I found the book containing a likeness to the piece she had created. I looked up and saw her looking at me around the corner of the book shelf, which I thought was weird of her. Her demeaner changed towards me after that. She spoke a lot of her fiancé proposing to her on the beach, and I kept wondering why she had never introduced him to me.

I was slow about it, but I eventually saw her as a user. When I realized she was relying on me to pay for her lunch every time we went out, I told her one day I could not afford hers. I saw her less and less until the day when she told me that if I didn't want to come to her wedding, it was okay. I did not attend, and we never saw each other again. I began to wonder just how easy I was. Or was I just plainly blind and didn't want to admit it. What struck me was not feeling hurt or angry.

Buddy

Buddy at about three months

My brother, Michael, had given us a dog he named Buddy. He was 85% German Shephard, 10% boxer, and 5% who knew what and 100% heart. He was a mutt – like me. That dog had a personality unlike any other dog I had ever known. He and Patrick used to fake-wrestle. Buddy would sound like he was literally tearing him apart, and someone actually came to the door to tell me that my dog was attacking my husband. Buddy also had the notion that no one was allowed to stay on the property unless he could knock them down, place a front paw on their chest and liberally wash their face.

When my mother came to live with us, she was aware of Buddy's antics, and did everything she could to prevent the face washing. It became a game between them that didn't last long. Two months after mom's arrival, I saw Buddy in the bushes near the porch and watched the scene unfold from the kitchen window. He had calculated when she would be outside. When he spotted her, he ran out, got between her legs and tripped her. But he was also fast enough to place himself between her the ground to help break her fall. Down and on her back, he quickly put his paw on her chest; and you could see him relish in the washing of her face. I will swear to this day, that dog was laughing when he ran off. My mother cussed while struggling to get up from the ground, but she was also smiling.

Over time, Buddy showed me how to play. I grew old at an early age and never really played as a child – never really understood play. Watching Buddy as a puppy showed me how play relaxed you, allowed you to have fun. We would let him loose on a daily basis to allow him to be his mischief self under our watchful eye. I am not sure if he ever "grew up." One day, I sat down on the grass and waited for him. When he spied me, he ran over and instinctively knew what to do. He sat down beside me and licked my cheek. I put my arm around his neck and soon we were "wrestling" as a human and a gentle dog could wrestle. After that, whenever I was in my overalls, we would wrestle and hug each other. Buddy taught me the pleasures and boundless joy of play and how to laugh.

His intelligence and compassion sometimes amazed me. Davy, his wife Ro, and their daughter, Amanda, came for a visit. My son was also there with our grandson Chris, along with my Michael and his partner, Ann. We were all out in the snowy yard walking around for a break from being indoors, thoroughly engrossed in our conversations. After a while, we adults went back indoors. About twenty minutes later, I hadn't heard the kids and asked where they were. No one had remembered them coming in. Panicked, everyone jumped up and put on their coats.

We ran outdoors, shouting the kid's names. We even went up the two-tract into Pa's meadow; all the while calling out their names. When we were back in our yard, Patrick got an idea and called out, "Buddy." Buddy poked his head out the large door of his square, home-made dog house. "Where are the kids?" Buddy's head disappeared, and a couple moments later, he stuck his head out again. The two missing kids jutted their heads out under his. We were all speechless as the two kids came out running and laughing with their arms outstretched. I will also swear that Buddy was smiling broadly at being a good babysitter. I sat with him for a while that night when giving him his dinner bowl with a little extra in it, along with a huge hug and loving words.

Buddy was also stubborn. He wanted what he wanted. Usually when I had overnight guests, I would cook biscuits and gravy for breakfast. In the evening, I would put the extra gravy on Buddy's dry food. One morning, I made pancakes for my guests and did not have any leftovers. That night, as I walked away after placing his bowl on the ground, Buddy let out a bark. I kept going a few steps. The bark got louder, like he was shouting. I looked back around at him. He tapped his bowl with his nose. I just stood there. He tapped his bowl again. I then understood and said so. Back in the kitchen, I cooked a small pan of gravy and took it out to him. "Okay?" I asked after emptying it into his bowl. His nodded his head and proceeded to eat. His understanding of the English language never ceased to amaze me.

Then there was the time Buddy kept getting loose, and I thought it was the neighbors freeing him. One day, I put the chain back on his collar and saw how the hoop worked and got curious. When I went back into the kitchen, I sat and watched. Buddy looked in both directions and stepped onto the cement block we over the fence to keep him from getting out. He moved his head against the fence in such a way; the chain was latched the fence and Buddy was loose. But was not enough. I watched as he went to the corner nudged the fence open and squeezed past the fence post. He then turned around and used his nose to push fence back in place. Then he ran to the neighbors who always gave Buddy butterscotch candy as a treat.

At thirteen Buddy started getting tumors on his back. In March, the veterinarian told us that his front legs could run, but the back ones could hardly get up. He suggested we put him down rather than let him suffer. He had been getting slower in the winter months before and seemed to tire easily; like his spunk had disappeared. About the same time, Patrick had his first heart attack and was in the Petoskey Heart Hospital, an hour's drive away. I knew I could not keep up with both of them and the house. So, I decided to put Buddy down a few months early. He and I talked about it, and I sensed he understood. Patrick convinced me to take Gil with me. I thought I could handle it, but did as he suggested. Good thing! The same vet Buddy had his entire life asked if I was sure I wanted to be in the same room, and I said, "He has always been there for me. I will be here for him."

Up until that point in time, I never reacted emotionally to much of anything, including Patrick's heart attack. I watched without emotion as the vet put the needle in Buddy's arm. In a few moments, he went down on the table. I was still fine until the vet used two fingers to close Buddy's eyes. I lost it. A box of tissue was handed to me, and Gil escorted me out the back door. I sobbed during the 20-minute drive home, and for another hour. My son was beside himself because he had never seen me like that before. Much to my surprise, Gil was very consoling. A different position for me. Afterwards, it occurred to me that sometimes Patrick was wiser than I.

PART IV
Empty Nest

Life Goes On

One of my favorite baskets

I converted the garage/store into a Fiber Art Studio. I created baskets from Birch bark, purchased reed, and gathered grape vines and prepped them for coiling or adding them to other creations. When I was weaving alone in my studio, my mind would slip into an altered state – got lost in it. Often, I would not remember how I wove a basket. They came out beautiful, smooth with no tiny "hairs" sticking out on any of the weavings. I still use the large laundry basket, and have kept the large oval basket I found my grandson sitting in one day. Both are over thirty years old.

One-woman art show

I learned wheat-weaving from a book. Loom weaving was part of the Fiber Art I class, so I bought a floor loom and made a portable loom and kept all of my work in my studio. A few pieces were sold occasionally until an acquaintance of mine had heard of my art. She owned a frame shop in Gaylord and talked me into a one-woman art show in her gallery. Much to my surprise, it was well received. Eventually, most of my art pieces were sold in other studios, or found their way across the US and the Virgin Islands.

My studio had been opened for a couple of years when I received a notice of a Fiber Art V class being offered by Central Michigan University. Even not taking Fiber II, III, or, IV, my Fiber Art instructor, Prof. Sally, gave me permission to register. I misread the length of the class and only took enough clothes to last a week. You guessed it. Due to lack of enough money, all the laundry was done in one load that turned out a soft pink because of a new red shirt. But it was okay. I learned a great deal more about myself during those two weeks.

The class was divided into two, with eight students in each class. The advance and established artists were in one class, with me and the beginners in the other class. No worries, as I enjoyed teaching. What was sad was the silent competition that went on between the two classes. I was somewhat oblivious in the beginning, until the advance group wanted to come into our classroom when I was teaching how to add potpourri and essential oils to the papermaking. Our class was never allowed in the advance class. Yet, our students had to barricade the door to our classroom to prevent the advance class from entering. I thought they had done it in fun, until I heard the noise from the other side.

My students and I had a talk, and I learned that some of them were not happy with being teased about my being the "only artist" in the room. I thought the whole thing childish and didn't feed into it. I finally convinced them that if they had not been good enough, Guidance would not have put them with me. Things did eventually settle down. When they did, I praised those around me, and pointed out how their work was unique and original.

Part of the class requirement was creating something by sculpting clay and molding Paper Mâché over it. I had never sculpted anything before, except with clay in my childhood. I put on my earphones and blocked out the world as I fashioned the clay under my hands. I got lost in envisioning the head of an old Native American Indian with a face filled with lines of wisdom, all-knowing eyes and long braids. After several hours, I came out of my altered state and took off my earphones. Imagine my shock at seeing a plain face with no eyes. I couldn't even bring myself to put hair on the sculpted head, and had to ask someone to use their lips as a model.

Oh Me' Ha- paper mâché mask

Two years after the Paper Mâché class, during a journey to the upper world, I met the individual owning the face I had sculpted. Her name is Oh Mae' Ha, standing about four feet tall, olive skin, with a head as bald as an egg. She is my acupuncture guide. The one who guided me where to sting people during bee venom sessions, or when I was doing Shiatsu massages. There is a crack in the chin of the paper mask, because I was too impatient to wait for the mask to totally dry, and it tore when removing the mask from the mold. Her facial image is hanging on my wall in an enclosed shadow box, surrounded by navy blue and blood-red shimmering fabrics. The tear in the mask stands as a reminder that patience is the least of my virtues.

In my second Paper Mâché project in the photo, the white commercial paper was made by macerating it in a blender. The pulp was drained on cloth screen then draped over the grey paper made from paper trash that was thrown into

Lake Michigan. The lake water macerates whatever paper is tossed into the water, then the waves toss it on shore as one piece of paper. I almost grabbed the one with the messed-up McDonald logo, but decided not to use it because of it representing commercialism. A dried mushroom from the sand is in the center. I am proud of that piece.

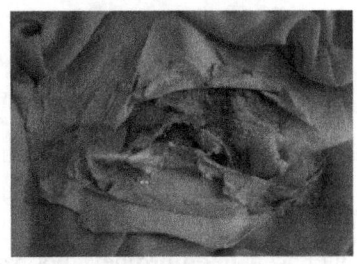

Paper mâché and dried mushroom

Beaver Island is accessible only by a two-hour ferry ride from the mainland. At the time, no personal vehicles were allowed on the island except for the one bus used for public transport, though bicycles were aplenty. We took a bus tour that included a house built solely from driftwood. My interest piqued; I got off the bus. The landscape to the house looked wild with plants in the sandy yard. The house itself had shingles cut from driftwood and placed everywhere on the outside – the roof, the siding, etc. Driftwood was also used inside the house for the bedframe, cabinets, etc. What tickled my humor was the bathroom door. When opened, it closed off the very small pantry. When you opened the pantry door with many small jars on shelves hanging on the door, you closed off the bathroom. I thought it clever, but I didn't think to check to see how the hinges were placed on the wall.

Everywhere there was driftwood, and I marveled at how the varnish exposed the intricate markings in the end tables, dining room table, bedframe and headboard. The kitchen cabinet doors showed how the lake water had sculpted away the ends of the wood, rounding them unevenly or looking like lace. It gave the kitchen an artistic feel. I was enthralled by and thoroughly enjoyed the couple who shared other artifacts, displayed in and around their home, that they had picked up in their global travels. I felt the whole home was an artistic masterpiece of a house - inside and out. It was one of the few times in my life I was in envy and in awe.

For those who lingered, the couple told a story about a man who appeared onshore of the island around 1900, or thereabouts. No one knew from where he came or how he got there, since no boat was found. He demonstrated his skills as a healer by using island plants in his potions and herbal remedies. He was well-liked but kept to himself. He never married and had no children. It is told that he enjoyed going down into the large bowl-shaped hole located in the center of the island to get many of his herbs. The bowl held many prehistoric-looking vegetation with very large leaves. He was the only who went down there, because the locals did not care for the bowl's eerie feel. He lived amicably on the island for about twenty years, until one day, he disappeared. No one knew how he left, as he still had no boat.

The papermaking class taught me how creatively gifted I was. I enjoyed taking natural fiber or plants, tearing them apart and creating something different. The art piece for my final grade was a small round paper book. I had used an embroidery hoop about eight inches in diameter to form the eight pages of potpourri paper. Each page had two holes that displayed the footprints on the next page. You had the impressions the feet were walking and had to turn the pages to see where the foot prints led you. A long twig along the side on the top page, sewn with fake sinew, held the book together. It was titled "My Prayer" with a prayer of protection on each page: one for peace, love, etc... Printed on the last page was, "God, please protect me from myself." The book sold for $45 at the Beaver Island Papermaking Art show held the day before we left.

During the one weekend of the class, Sally pulled me aside and asked me to look at a recipe in a large papermaking book. After reading it, I told her the recipe had no cellulose, the natural glue in the plant that held fibers together. The recipe was flawed and said so. She thought the same. Then I said, "Why ask me?" Becca had told her of my one-woman art show, and Sally felt confident I could confirm her thoughts about the recipe. It was then I felt I had graduated from novice artist to pro.

I didn't stay with the art of papermaking for very long. That is the case for PTSD victims. They don't usually stay long with most things, be it a relationship with a person, a thing, accomplishments, etc. And it seemed that once I accomplished a thing, I was done with it. Sometimes, feeling something accomplished was fulfilling enough and didn't need the continual feeding.

During this same time, I attended Kirtland Community college for computer classes and received a certificate for Word Processing Specialist.

Unexpected Blessing

On one particular day I walked out the back door, and the apple blossom fragrance was so strong, it nearly turned my stomach. And per his usual quirky timing, this was a day Patrick felt "frisky." We usually responded to our sexual desires, and this day was no different. We got down under a tree at the top of the steps, me on the ground feeling the prickly Creeping Phlox we had planted on the bank. He was on top, feeling the lower branch of the bush-tree above him, sticking his butt every time he lifted it. What happened during the next few minutes was something I had never before experienced.

Flower seen during altered state

My eyes were closed during the heat of our passion. As I entered into an altered state, I smelled an exotic vanilla-perfume like fragrance. Slowly appearing in this altered state was a vision of a pale blue, six-starred flower with black lines running from top to bottom of each petal, with an unusual yellow-orange center. I knew the fragrance came from the flower and wondered, on some level of consciousness, how it had over-powered the Apple blossoms. They both stayed with me until my climax, when both slowly faded. I was surprised that I had not heard Patrick during all of this. Nor did I feel the wind blowing on us, as it had in the beginning. It never occurred to us that people could see us from the road, until after we stood up and got dressed. Hearing the cars, we chuckled in embarrassment.

The flower's image and fragrance never left me. For many years I could still "smell" the exotic vanilla-perfume-like fragrance. I searched for the flower on the computer, in the library, in local gardens. Even the botanical gardens were checked when we traveled to Canada – to no avail. One day, Becca and I went to visit her artist friend. While they talked, I moved around his studio looking at his amazing paintings, when I came across a covered easel. I did the unforgivable and lifted the covering. When I opened my eyes, I was looking up into the eyes of my frantic friend and host.

Helping me up, the artist looked at the easel then back at me. He smiled, pointing to the easel, and he asked, "You have seen that flower before?" Taking up most of the canvas was the exact same flower in my vision, down to the same blue shade. I nodded my head, still surprised and embarrassed by my faint. He shared that he only knew of two others who had seen it, one from Japan and the other from Germany. He was British. I shared that I could not find the flower anywhere in my years of research. He related that I would not find it in our reality. *Our reality?* He caught me falling backwards. I was feeling foolish at not being to handle things. My body felt hot and weak, and my heart raced.

He and Becca helped me to a soft chair. He asked if it smelled like vanilla and exotic perfume. I nodded again, still speechless. He went on to explain, "It is a rare blessing to see and smell such a flower from another reality. It is a flower witnessed during true passion of love and joy, mainly joy." I didn't think to ask him how he knew this to be a fact. I copied this flower in the back of my book, *My Journey to Peace with PTSD,* published in 2007. I think I will smell this flower for the rest of my life. The experience at the time showed me I had been given an unusual gift that would guide me to the most amazing part of myself.

After mom's and Buddy's deaths, I felt lost for a while and worked at many jobs, including flower arranging at a flower shop. Though I did enjoy working at STT Company doing inventory for local mom and pop stores and large grocery chains. Genie, my boss, and I did a lot of the small stores together. I began working in offices as computer operator for Kelly Services again – a few days here, a few days there. This kept up for a few years, all the while feeling a little lost.

I tried my hand at writing; had always enjoyed it. A small fire was lit under me, and I submitted a short story. But Patrick put a stop to wherever that would have taken me. It was about this time in our marriage, when I began to become suspicious of some of his behavior. During a friends' visit at our house, he made small derogatory comments about me. When I mentioned his making the comments, he denied them. Friends stopped coming over, and I started meeting them elsewhere. Otherwise, Patrick and I went back to our schedule of putting wood in the wood shed, my cooking, cleaning, and all the other mundane tasks a homemaker does.

But I still wondered about Patrick's behavior. I began relating his behavior to those of the abusers I had learned about while working as office manager of a shelter in Grayling that housed women and children of Domestic abuse. I talked a lot with the psychologist working there. I lasted there for a year before being hired as an office supervisor for a company that made annealed copper tubing. I went into what I thought was a clerk's job, and discovered I was the left hand to the president/owner of the company. I had been hired by CJ, Human Relations, who would often come up from the second owned company down state.

The president talked to me occasionally, and I made the mistake of relating this to CJ. For the first time in my life, I was fired before a month's end of work. I saw CJ six months later at the Farmer's Market. She informed me that she "gotten a divorce and married the boss," meaning the owner of the multi-million-dollar company. Recognizing the "So, there!" attitude in her saunter as she walked away told me why I had been fired. She was afraid I was after the boss. I learned later that the factory people were not happy with her. I was at peace with the firing.

In July, 1995, we were in the woods searching for what we could find to cut for firewood when I saw snow under some of the trees. When we first moved our mobile home to Gaylord, there were only 84 days between spring and fall frosts. We had experienced a very hard and long winter in 1994/1995. But finding snow in the woods in July was too much. I turned to Patrick and he said, "I know. We're moving."

PART V
New Beginning

Sneedville, Tennessee

On state Highway 32 in Hancock County, Sneedville, Tennessee, we found 12.3 acres with a very small creek at the bottom of a steep gully. Sneedville is hidden on the north side of Clinch Mountain's Kentucky/Tennessee border. I truly thought I was moving closer to my birth state of Kentucky, and had visions of visiting relatives I had never met. After having purchased our first riding mower, my husband found his lounge chair and never left it. I am a strong-minded woman with the strength of a man, so I went to building our new homeplace by myself. He did help with the roof trusses for the Dome. But, otherwise, I was left to do the work.

I learned how to mow more than an acre of lawn on a steep slope, with me leaning far to one side or the other to balance the mower. A bulldozer cut a house seat in the middle of a long, slopped hill, upon which we first built a 12'x16' guest house. We lived in that guest house until the 40' wide Monolithic Dome was built. A small well house was built with a greenhouse attached to it later. The paved driveway ran about 200' down to Highway 31. I loved my home, but the Dome not only perplexed the community, but also my building it. A lot of the men just couldn't tolerate my doing the building and told me, "No woman should lift a hammer."

I responded, "Show me where the penis is, and I will put the hammer down." Well, you can pretty much guess where things went from there with the good-ol' boys.

I am knowledgeable in a lot of things, but was not allowed to get involved into community work. It took a couple of years to learn about three brothers ran the town. The oldest one owned the hardware store and was mouthier, giving the impression he was the one in charge. The second brother owned the lumber yard and was the quiet one; but the one actually in charge. The third went on to become a State Representative; and seemed content as long as he had his moonshine.

The town judge was known as "cokehead." You got the impression that those working in the courthouse worked for the three brothers more than for the town's residents. One of the ways the powers-at-be controlled the town was allowing the farmers to buy their seed from the hardware store on credit; along with anything else they needed. When the crop was harvested, they paid off their credit. The same with the lumber store. Everything but groceries was provided between the two stores. The three brothers also governed the school system. Any government funding that came into the county for education, medical, etc. was skimmed off the top and divided among the brothers. When I had heard from a reliable source that one of the brothers was seen sitting in a fast-food restaurant viewing a medical patient's file, I found another doctor in another town.

Patrick and the back patio porch I built.
Guest house is to the left.

The other hardware store was run by three younger brothers, just trying to make a living. This is the store where I did most of my business. I had gone into the older store looking for someone to help me build, and they laughed at me. I was told, "What are you going to do, now that you don't have anyone to work fer ya?"

I retorted, "I guess I am going to have to do what you guys don't have the balls to do." And they laughed and laughed.

Folks eventually learned that you don't mess with The Lady. We hired someone to build the cement wall and 2' foundation for the Dome. I purchased books on electrical wiring and plumbing before the guest house was built, so knew what I wanted to do with the Dome. Most of the plumbing was done before the cement work was done on the Dome's foundation. The hidden electrical and plumbing had to be done before the walls were gunited (cement mixture sprayed on the walls). I even rented a transit level to find the eight openings for the windows and two doors. The foundation was 40' across with 2' footers at the outer edges that gradated to 6" of cement across the center. Under this cement was 1" insulated foam, a square rebar grid, and double-grid work of 5/8" rebar in a circular pattern across all of it. I learned a lot more in construction as I did the work. Another person was hired to buff out the cement foundation after it was poured and dried.

It took two days to set the plastic Dome cover in place and adhere it to the foundation before it was blown up. Another three days to gunite the interior wall. A neighbor built the "jig" that helped us to build the 12"x 20" trusses for the second-floor beams. We built the inner walls and used 6,000 shear bolts to hold the ceiling beams onto the cement walls. I was truly thankful for my building skills and manly strength. After the cement guniting, but before interior walls were completed, I moved into our Dome before the inspection because the guest house became too comfortable. After the final inspection, I walked into that older store and found the same group of men had who laughed at me. They were all lolling around the counter, which is typical of a country store. I asked, "Gentleman, what do you think now that there is a woman who can do a job you couldn't do?" They all turned their backs on me. I walked out smiling.

Being Hard

For several years many men made passes at me, including a few preachers. This kept me from going to some public places for socializing. I never understood the community's animosity toward me, but found that it fed my core's anger. This anger had been carried throughout my life and stayed hidden; but it started to surface. The realization was slow in coming, as I understood why I often took up the challenges made by the locals. The gossip was, they simply didn't know what to do with me. I was a female, a rebel, not religious and didn't need to hire anyone, since I could do a man's work. I was a phenomenon they wanted to be rid of. I learned that the women were taking notice of my courage and strength, and that made me a threat to the men. The men wanted their womenfolk complacent and obedient, and didn't want me teaching their womenfolk.

No one complained about the tires I had collected and stacked on the property until I started putting them on the bank and filling them with dirt to help with erosion. The county inspector came by and said I couldn't do it, that it was against EPA regulations. With him standing inside the doorway, I picked up the phone book, called EPA and asked about the tires on the bank. They said it was an excellent idea. "Would you please tell that to this gentleman?" and handed the phone to the inspector. In a belligerent tone, he declined to talk to the man. He said he would remove the tires and take them away. One truck went over the mountain in the direction of the dump site, which I knew to be illegal. The second truck went in the other direction toward town. I later learned that the EPA office for our area was in Georgia. I had called Knoxville, TN. That one made me smile for quite a while.

Other occasions would arise when I had to get hard with some of the "leaders." The final day came when I walked into Bea's restaurant at lunch time. Bea and I had become friends soon after I moved to town. I had sat at the remaining empty table next to a round table of eight men in suits. A few minutes later, I overhead a man sitting right next to my chair saying, "Women are so stupid with so much crap in their brains, you can't even push a maggot through their ears." Then the speaker turned to me and said, "Ain't that right? Huh? Ain't that right," and nudged my elbow a second time while broadly grinning. Everyone at the table laughed, along with a few others in the restaurant.

I calmly turned to him and said, "You would like me to tell you what you think of women?" It was my turn to smile.

"Yes, ma'am. You tell me." And everyone laughed again. Bea chuckled as she got up from her chair and walked into the kitchen.

"Your women put supper on the table at the end of the day. And they do your laundry."

"Amen." I knew then that they were preachers.

"They raise your children, keep your house clean, and take care of your animals and crops on the farm?"

"Amen," laughing louder.

"And they spread their legs to allow you to fornicate. Provided, of course, you are not over the other side of the ridge fornicating with someone else's wife. Ain't that right? Huh? Huh?" And I pointed a finger at the man on the other side of the round table. "You made a pass at me only last week." Except for Bea's laughter in the kitchen, you could hear a pin drop. That was the last time I was verbally accosted in public. I never cared for behaving like a bitch, so I stayed to myself after that, hoping it wouldn't happen again.

Needing something to do and to get away from the Dome, I worked part-time for a woman who did sheet-rock finishing. When she found out I could also do carpentry work, she added that skill to my jobs. I put a stop to it when she had me climbing a ladder to the second floor to repair a dormer because I am afraid of heights. We also did electrical work after she learned I did my own. One thing I did not like about the job was, even though she asked me to be on the job early, we often didn't leave early because she had to smoke her weed. I did enjoy some of her parties.

Surreal Life

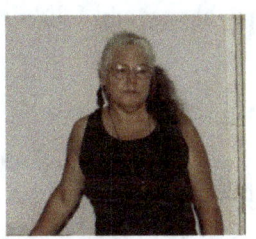
1998

While building the Dome, I had an on-and-off affair with a local man for about seven years. He embodied the wildness I craved while we met at various places where we would not be noticed. He was brazening at times, when we were together in public. This concerned me, lest we got caught. I loved him for the traits Patrick didn't have.

My personality changed. At 55 years old, I took a job at a truss company as chop-saw operator and worked alongside of seven other younger men. My strength kept surprising me as I lifted sixteen-foot boards and pulled the heavy cart of heavy chopped boards to the miter saw. Time passed while I worked in my gardens and taught myself masonry. I built two 150' walls out of anything and everything I could put my hands on. Both walls were about 3' tall and 5' apart and curved the property.

Lady's wild side, age 55

After moving to Tennessee, I found my wild side when going on my own, escaping for the first time without rules or supervision. I went 4-wheeling with my mechanic and a couple of his crew members with my Suzuki and smoked pot. Weed made me feel I had no control over my feelings, but still tried one more time and did not like it. This was before the flashback that took away all control of myself. Everything in my life during this time led up to the final breakdown.

I planted irises all across the front of the bottom wall. It was a beautiful site of 150' of tall, large yellow irises. Many cars would slow down, as they watched this white-haired, elder female build all of this. They watched her standing on the Dome, painting it pale blue, and building the two porches. One porch was built about 40'long, curved next to but not connected to the Dome. I didn't want to connect to the Dome's cover lest holes were put into the Dome's skin. Any rain falling off the Dome ran into a 2' stone moat around the Dome's perimeter and out to the drain ditch next to the road.

I enjoyed myself at this time of my life while Patrick sat in his lounge chair; doing nothing to help me in any of the yard work. He did do one thing that surprised me. He got disability for his knee that had been affected by the polio he contracted when he was fourteen. The money eased a lot of our financial problems, and I didn't have to work for the truss company any more.

Counseling Again

I helped Robin with remodeling her house. She was a young woman working as a CPA for a bank in another county. I did her sheetrock finishing and other little things. My son tried to get involved with her, but I did my best to discourage their union. His fourth wife had just divorced him, and I knew his personality. He turned part of her attic into an office, with pull-out steps to reach it. When he tried to turn things into competitions, I worked when he was not around.

I also counseled her because of the abusive boyfriend she had before moving from Georgia. He had dropped a stove pipe on her eye and nearly took it out. He stalked her with constant phone calls about every ten minutes throughout the day and evening. I could still feel his car behind my vehicle driving at 60 mph on a major highway just to keep him from getting between my car and hers. I knew he wanted to really harm her.

We tried getting a restraining order. Not succeeding with our residential county judge, which I am sure was because of me, we obtained one from the county in which she worked. I knew her abuser had received his restraining order by mail when her landline stopped ringing. It was eerie standing in her quiet bedroom. He didn't call again. The court hearing kept being postponed, and it took over a year to get before a judge. When I stood up in front of the judge and demanded he stop postponing the hearing, in a testy voice, he responded, "If I have to postpone again, it will be because my leg is broken. Will that suffice?"

"Yes, your honor, it will. And I thank you." We won our case a month later. I saw the judge at a VA function a few weeks late; and to his credit, he came over and asked how she was doing. I commended him for what he had done, and told him she was doing well. I apologized for my behavior, and he said it was alright. That he understood someone had to fight for her. The judge had made a similar remark in the courtroom when the other attorney had told Robin to read only a certain section of the document he had given her before the hearing. I had told her to read the whole thing.

Not long afterwards, Robin became pregnant. A medical issue put her in the hospital at five months of pregnancy. My son took that time to tell her that he would no longer be seeing her. It was also when Robin told me that my son had suggested they date and not tell me, to which she agreed. That cooled my heart on both of them. While being with her every step during the pregnancy, Robin's mother gradually came back into the picture. The day she went into labor, I drove her mother over the mountain roads at 80 mph and met the ambulance at the ER. I was told it would be several hours before delivery, so, I took the time to get a haircut, grateful to be able to relax. When I got back to the hospital, they were sewing her up after delivering a baby boy. Intuition told me that I was going to lose my "daughter" and new grandson.

Being a premature baby, Phoenix stayed in the hospital for a few weeks longer. I held him for a few minutes when he was about three weeks old. A few hours later, Robin's mother gave me hell for holding the baby. The nurse came in at that time and was also very upset because I didn't have their natural blood and were afraid that I could give "something" to the baby. I was hurt. I wanted to comment about the adopted babies. Instead, I distanced myself from Robin and her mother, and they seemed pleased. Many years later, Robin came to visit me in North Carolina. I sensed what she wanted, but I couldn't give it to her. I had walked away and couldn't go back.

I began to realize at this juncture of my life that people would come to me, needing my help, and I would accommodate them. When I was no longer needed, we would separate. This taught me that we have relationships based on the needs of one or the other, or both parties involved. When the need or needs have been satisfied, the relationship dissolves. I am not sure if this anesthetized me to people, keeping me at a distance; or I just plainly didn't get deeply involved because I knew it would not be permanent. In some ways there is a sense of freedom of knowing there would be no ties. But on a different level, I also found it a little lonely.

Changing My Tune

March 15, 1998, Ordination Ceremony

Someone mentioned there was a group of strange people in a nearby town called "Jesus freaks." I got curious and went looking for them. The retreat and religious community of The Science of Spirituality and Healing was not what I had expected. I got to know the Director and his staff, and a few months later, I took their ministry course. A year later, after proving my skills with Intuition and Discernment (psychic abilities) and hands-on healing, I was ordained. My friendship with Bill, the founder, and the community lasted a few more years before I moved out-of-state. I will mention here that I received my first massage from Albert, a medicine man who had visited South America twice a year for many years to work with Shamans. I also met a Lakota Shaman, Braveheart. He and Bill did not really get along well, as Bill was manipulative. Women often fell in love with Bill, but I did not.

While working within the ministry, I had agreed to do a vision quest. The quests are used to discern one's future, as a rite of passage, look for deep, profound answers, etc... I had never done a quest before and was truly curious. On the highest part of the mountain of the property, a circle was created with stones. There would be no food and no water the day before and for as long as I was on the quest. Ceremony and prayers were done. If I had to void myself, it was done outside the circle. It did not rain during the two days, which was good, as I laid on the blanket in the circle during the whole time.

I watched the sky on the first day with no thoughts running through my head. When I pondered this, I found it profound, because my head had always been filled with "stuff." At some point in the afternoon, I entered into an altered state. I don't even remember it getting dark or falling asleep. The second day, I distinctly remember seeing the sun rise, the sun moving across the sky above me then setting. And I will swear it only took ten minutes from sunrise to sunset. Thoroughly amazed, I was not all sure what alternate universe I was in. I didn't know when I fell asleep or when it got dark. Had I been drinking I would have sworn someone had slipped something in my beverage. I did not feel it was a hallucination, nor was I nervous or scared. I actually felt protected. The next day, I awoke and intuitively knew my vision quest was done. I packed up everything, said my prayers of gratitude and walked down to the lodge. Everyone was waiting, and I shared what had happened but had no message to share with them. Everyone but Bill was disappointed. I did learn that he had prayed in a loud voice most of the time I was up on the mountain.

After meeting a couple of gay men in their home, I became aware that I was being discussed among the community. When I went to put my hands out in front to sense the new tiles framing their fireplace, they both jumped at my hand to gently remove it. Responding to the question on my face, one of them said, "We are aware of your abilities and have seen them." I knew nothing of what they were talking about; but in time the realization would slowly come. My abilities would make me a loner for the rest of my life, that people would treat me differently. Some with great respect and awe, others with fear. But always honored. No longer did I help anyone, unless they asked. One should always get permission to help or assist, unless asked. The question puts people in a receptive mode. Even asking someone with a disability if they want or need assistance, you are saying that you are seeing their presence and not their disability.

More talents came to light, and I learned to just accept them and wait. There were a couple of times when I saw a person's face in my mind, I would stop what I was doing and get dressed. All the while I'm am dressing, I am complaining about having to go out after 7 PM, the starting of my evening downtime. The drive was invariably twenty minutes. I'd walk in the door at the right moment and ask, "Why am I here?" Over time, others would come to me for future readings. But those readings stopped when I learned people had based their decisions on the readings, thereby changing the reading's outcome, rather than allowing the future to unfold.

People would sometimes drain me when getting close to me, or try to use me. Those people were bipolar. On learning the reasons for their relationship, I'd let them ago, sometimes without telling them why. My strength and courage were just a couple of reasons people were attracted to me, so, I became cautious. I learned that I was considered an exotic, because I was so different. Always having been lied to during my youth, transparency became very important to me. I knew how the lies felt, and didn't want anyone else to hurt. When people asked me questions, and I knew the answers would hurt, I would say so. People don't really want to hear the truth, and I didn't want to explain. But when they pressed me, I would do my best to gently tell them, then walk away.

The Accident

A 4-wheel-drive Suzuki, christened Suzi, was my vehicle of choice, and I learned to drive a 5-speed. I loved her. I got her for a cheap price because the seller couldn't get the speed past 40 mph. Tony, my mechanic, accidently spotted the problem, when he had the hood up with the engine running. She ran beautifully after he fixed the problem. She got my butt into trouble, and she got me out of it. My husband was not happy with my driving her all over the place, because I was away from home a lot. In 1999, he constantly nagged me to sell her. I got tired of our arguments and sold Suzi. We bought a used Ford Frontier pickup at an auction with nearly bald tires. We thought we could wait a while for new tires.

A couple of weeks later, on a hot day with drizzling rain, I made a slight left turn. The truck did not hold the road and kept going straight, in what seemed like slow-motion, for the longest time. It went across a front yard, across a short field then into a rather deep ditch. My head hit the driver door window before it impacted the windshield, breaking my eye glasses. One of the "unbreakable" lenses broke in half, cutting my right eye lid. The membrane between the eyelid and eyeball had not been cut. I remember someone putting a chain on the axle to keep the truck from flipping onto its roof. The axle was bent and the cab leaned toward the engine; totaling the truck. A helicopter flew me from ER in Morristown to the UT Hospital in Knoxville. The neurosurgical team cut me from sternum to hairline to find the bleeder that caused my veins to collapse. An inch and a half of my small intestines were removed.

I thought I was in ICU for three days, but learned that it had been four. I was not in this reality during the first day. While traveling with my Guide on the in a twilight place, we passed rooms with closed doors. I heard many people whispering in one of the closed rooms. While moving, I constantly felt something like a whisper or feather barely brushing my arms. In the next moment, I found myself standing alone in front of a counsel of twelve men, sitting at a glistening, somewhat transparent, round table. Everything around them was pale blue and white, like there was a light coming from somewhere. It was not exactly a room, but a very open space. And I don't remember standing on a "floor."

I recognized Bo sitting at the head of the council. Bo is short for a very long name I still cannot spell out and always miss one syllable when pronouncing it. A year before, he was the one who had walked into the room where Bill was giving me a massage. When I had asked who was the spirit that walked into the room with him, Bill described Bo exactly. He stood in the corner of the massage room and introduced himself, then went out the door when someone had opened it. Time on the other side of the veil is always NOW. There is no past, present, or future, unlike our linear time. Bo was there for a reason.

I stood before the council and nodded to each out of respect, though Bo was the only one I could describe. He said, "Lady, if you feel you cannot handle what you think is the monumental task in front of you, you don't have to go back." I don't recall making the choice as I came to in ICU lying on a cold, metal table. Today, in my memory, I can still see the glass table and the twelve figures with Bo at the head.

A week after my discharge, I saw the dentist for the follow-up on my eye surgery. The idea of a dentist sewing my eye angered me, until he said that he was also a Maxillofacial surgeon. I had asked why he waited until I was in recovery to sew me up. He matter-of-factly responded, "There's no point in sewing up a corpse. And your eye was like sewing mop ends." That was sobering, to say the least, and left me quiet in thought for several days. My accident had blocked my long-term memory, except the three people who visited me in the hospital. I was told that many people called the hospital, and were told I was "seriously critical." The next step down was death.

More Spiritual Doors Open

My life changed dramatically after that auto accident. My past memory was like a puzzle, with jagged edges that had to be pieced together. My home didn't feel like my home. It was familiar and unfamiliar at the same time. I would recognize people, but would not remember what kind of relationship we had. This kept me cautious and mute. It was nerve-wracking at times. Two and a half years would pass when regaining some of my long-term memories became like Swiss cheese, through which I would drag memories or information.

A lot of unusual events occurred during those two and a half years. Like the one crossing a five-lane highway and looking to my right to see a very small car and its driver staring back. Our eyes locked, and our bumpers missed by inches, as was shown in my side mirror – all happening in slow motion with neither of us changing our speed. We were actually surprised to see each other, likely thinking we both had appeared out of thin air. Another incident was when I called my husband into the bedroom one night, and asked if he could see the bright light on a flower on the bank about eight feet from the window. He could not. It was there. I saw it shining like a tiny LED light.

I was not then and am not now a religious person. I have always been and still am a Spiritualist. Not many people really understand the term at its core. It is more than being able to communicate with spirits. Spiritualists have one law: We love everything, everywhere at all times, which defines God. Christians say they believe this, but they give me weird looks when I tell them that their coffee table is part God. To define the Dual Universe, it isn't just that the wood is part God. The actual wood decays back into the earth while the wood's invisible energy, or the essence of the wood created by electrons moving around the nucleus of an atom, wanders around the Universe. God is the totality of Universal energy, be it real material or atomic energy. It is as complicated as it is simple.

If one's belief is strong enough, they will be able to hear "angels" or guides talk to them. I prefer to think of it as being "compelled" with images rather than speech. And it also has to do with the energy level of both you and the guide communicating with you; which is another topic of discussion. I was always discovering new abilities and had reached the point of accepting them, deeming them as normal; and waited to see what I was supposed to do with them.

Six months after the 1999 accident, while driving on a mountain road, Guidance told me to move over. I was in the process of sliding over to the passenger side of the seat, when I realized I was driving – and in the wrong lane. I heard Guidance say in what seemed like a firm, slightly louder voice, "Lady, move over." I spotted a place on the shoulder. Just as I pulled into it, a car came around the curve and passed me. *That could have been one helluva wreck.*

Quite shaken, I just sat there trying to calm my body and my emotions. That was the first time I actually *heard* Guidance speak, never mind loudly. When I am "compelled," it comes from my core, not my brain, heart, or anywhere else; like a strong intuition. There is no other way to describe it, but as a strong sense of "knowing." My car parked, Guidance compelled, "Ask your questions." I had not shared much of my experiences of where my spirit went after the accident with anyone. But I always did have two questions.

Sitting on the shoulder of that quiet mountain road, I asked, "Who was whispering in the room in the twilight space?"

"Those were prayers for you," Guidance whispered in Its bass voice.

"And what was touching my arm moving the air above it?"

"Those were loving thoughts," came the gentle response.

"And the twilight place?"

"A place where some people go before they cut the soul cord to separate from the body."

"Thank you," I whispered.

I sat on the shoulder of that mountain road and bawled like a baby for nearly a half an hour. My residential community never really accepted me. So, I was curious who would love me and would pray for me, beyond a handful of people I knew. That mountain top cry was the last time I was able to cry real tears. It was many months before it occurred to me to ask who was responding to me. I had always received only two or three words from Guidance. The door that had opened during the accident will no longer stay closed. I had stepped onto another spiritual level.

Court Hearing

We needed a metal building and Marty, one of the brothers in the newer hardware store, had put me in touch with someone selling them. I ordered a 30'x40' for our garage and office space, but could not get the seller to give me a delivery date. My son needed to know when to come to erect it. I called daily for about three days to cancel and could not reach him. I called one more time and cancelled the order through a message before ordering another building from a local dealer. The original seller came a few days later and told me when it would come, and I reminded him of my many calls and message. He said his phone was not working. Gil came and erected the building with a partition containing a door, spacing off a 16' area for my office containing two windows.

About two weeks later, I walked into Marty's store. He showed me a document indicating he was being sued. The hearing was on September 11,

2001. On the day of the hearing, I went into courtroom to support Marty. After sitting down, I learned that I, too, was being sued. The judge asked if I had been served a warrant. "You know I wasn't, Bill" I was angry and arrogant. Everyone considered the notification given to me in court as my being served. Then the hearing was put off until after lunch the same day.

Deciding to visit a friend until the time of the hearing, I walked into her restaurant and watched on TV a plane bombing a tower. When asked, I was told it was not a horror movie, but was actually happening. This was the day the two towers went down in New York indicating it was not going to be a good day.

When I went back to the courtroom after lunch, I found it had been cleared of everyone except for those involved in the hearing with closed doors. Bill, the "cokehead," asked if it was okay that he not recuse himself as judge, even though he was also the attorney for the plaintiff. I agreed, just to get it out of his court. No one knew of my work experience in the courtroom.

The plaintiff won that hearing, as expected. When I walked out of the courtroom, I filled out an appeal document so old, it was yellow. An out-of-town attorney appealed the case, with a judge from the same county. I won the appeal. It cost me $75 more than if I had paid for the building; but I will always pay extra to fight a principle. What they did to me was wrong. I filed a complaint against the judge to the State Judiciary Committee in the State of Tennessee, and received a letter sighting thirteen violations committed by the "cokehead" judge/attorney.

Shortly after, I received another letter from the State's Attorney General office stating the case had been dismissed, with no reason given. When I called the state office and gave only my first name, I heard the person on the other end of the line swallow. He said they had not been given a reason. I later learned that the "cokehead" was the fair-haired child of the States's Attorney General when they practiced law together. My point had been made; but unfortunately, that was not the end of it.

Concerned that the brain was not healing as it should, I consulted a neurologist. He told me that brain cells die, but new ones are always regenerated and can take longer than two years. He also said to work on mind games to help the renewed cells. To keep my brain sharp, I became addicted to Free Cell.

I had opened up an office in the back of the new 30'x40' garage and put in a desk with a computer. I spent many hours doing a lot of research on everything and anything. I tried to start a non-profit with a Board to help kids, using our property as a day camp. The community was not having any of it. I walked away from that and the community; just cloistered up and stayed to myself.

I tried to get back into my Fiber Art by warping my floor loom. Staring at the wall with the large shelf unit with numerous kinds of yarns and accessories, I wondered what happened to my passion for Fiber Art. I tried writing again, but the words would not travel from my brain to the keyboard. Something major had changed within me, and I could not discern what it was. My days were filled with aimless thoughts, but I did stay home. I was not happy with Patrick not calling Gil to tell him about the accident. Had I died, Gil would have lost the opportunity to say goodbye. It convinced me that Patrick was a controlling person who did not want to share me with anyone, including our son.

In April, 2003, I took a 3-day course in Redirecting Children's Behavior. I garnered more information on children and was able to psychologically classify them. I found it curious that a lot of the adults could be classified into the same categories. I laughed out loud when I learned there was a course in Redirecting Corporate America. I did not take that one. I worked in Corporate America for over twenty years and knew how it behaved.

PART VI
Life Reveals Itself

Flashback

Saturday, August 8, 2003, Patrick, our son and grandson went golfing. I went out to my studio to plumb the sink with an elbow drain pipe that would take maybe 20–30 minutes and a job I had done many times before. When I got down and under the sink, my brain wouldn't function properly. I don't know why I felt I had to turn the water off, but couldn't remember where the turnoff valve was. I don't remember picking up the coping saw or why I even had it. Without thinking, I cut the cold-water pipe and was shocked when the water started gushing out onto me and the floor. I did have the wherewithal to run to the Dome and pull the breaker to the well.

The next seven hours were spent in an unknown numbed mental and emotional space cleaning up buckets after buckets of water with a mop; wringing the mop over and over again. I remember thinking that the number of times I wrung that mop during those hours seemed to total the number of times I had wrung a mop in my lifetime. When I went back to the sink to finish the plumbing job, I saw the turnoff valve to the cold water and turned it off. In my mind, it had not been there before, and still didn't fully understand why I had to turn the water off. I would have to fix the water pipe with a coupling, so it will wait. I then went into the Dome and pulled the breaker to the well and went to the task of cooking dinner for four – still in a numb state.

The next day the men went golfing again, leaving me to clean up the studio. Nothing was said to them. I could smell the dampness when I opened the studio door. When I had bent down to scrape something off the tiled floor, the tile disappeared before my eyes. I then saw the cement floor of the laundry room on my Naval base in Charleston. Shock does not begin to describe how I felt as I stood up and saw the rows of the deep sinks lining the wall. The image fading away, I found myself standing in front of a motel room door. *God, please don't let go into that room.* I no sooner had the thought when I stood on the other side of the door. My brain could not understand what was happening and wondered if I had entered another universe or a time warp.

I saw my unconscious body lying face down on the bed. There was blood everywhere – on my body, the bed and the rug. I then recalled my date had handed me a drink. When it was half gone; I became dizzy. He saw my condition and roughly turned me around, bent me over, pushed up my skirt.... I felt the pain in my vagina. As I watched myself gratefully passing out, the outside door was suddenly kicked open, and my friend Bubba came in. I knew a large amount of time had passed in only a few moments, while I stood there, watching everything. He saw my body and gently picked me up like a baby. While wrapping a sheet around me, he sympathetically cooed me, like one holding a hurt child.

The pain in my groin had me on my knees while the tiles on my studio floor reappeared again. I cried out when trying to stand, my vagina hurting so bad. I stayed on my knees until the pain subsided enough for me to move again. Using my hands to slowly push myself up from the floor, still groaning, the pain lessened. By the time I got to the Dome and to the phone, the pain had turned into a dull ache. I punched in the number. When she answered, I said, "Okay, Bobbie, I will go to the VA." When she asked what happened, I told her. She explained that I had had a flashback of a 40-year suppressed memory. I didn't want Patrick to take me, so, Bobby got someone else to escort me to the hospital. I didn't know what to tell him, and I didn't want to have to deal with his incessant questions.

Even today, I still wonder at my emotional and mental state and barely remembered walking through the ER. Forty minutes later, escorted by an attendant with a firm grasp on my shoulders, I walked into the Psychiatric Ward. Once on the other side of the door, two nurses appeared out of nowhere and gave me a very tiny pill and a small cup of water. When I asked what it was, I was told I didn't have to take it. "Are you kidding. Look at me." I didn't recognize the voice that hollered at them. I was trembling and scared of not knowing what was happening to me. I don't remember much after that and spent my first evening in lockdown; a place where someone observes you for 24 hours from a window in the wall above the bed.

The following morning, I awoke in a small single cot and rolled over to see five people quietly, patiently sitting in a semi-circle around my bed. I wondered how long they had been sitting there. Looking at my maroon-colored pajamas, I wondered who had dressed me or if I did it myself. I didn't see my clothes anywhere. In a voice not sounding like mine, I said, "I don't know what you have in mind, but I have to be out of here in a few days." They sat silently looking back at me with expressionless faces. I tried again, "Look. I'm okay. I had a good night's sleep…" Again, silence. "Okay, I was nervous yester…" Still nothing. I knew it was useless so I acquiesced. "You want to talk. Okay, so maybe I have a problem."

With that admission, the doctor said, "Mrs. Cerelli, we are your psych team and will be available 24/7 while we help you get through this." After telling me what to expect during my week's stay, they escorted me out to the main ward. Shown to my room, I was told they would be back. With nothing to do but wait, I walked out into the hall and read a poster on the wall. When I crossed the 14' hall and read a different poster, I realized I had totally forgotten the poster on the previous wall and just stood there, stunned. Before the 1999 accident, I could remember names, phone numbers, and dates from six months before. Now, I could not remember what I had just read two minutes earlier across a 14' hall. I got scared, confused, and nervous, all at once. Something was happening to me, and I could not control it. Could not stop it. Not having control angered me.

The flashback made me feel that my previous forty years had been a living lie. It was daunting to think that I had to rebuild a new life, simply because I could not remember the old one. On top of not knowing how much of my long-term memory I had regained; I discovered a flashback radically affects the short-term memory. This put me on another level of fear. The rest of the week was spent talking to doctors about medication, counseling and meeting other ward residents.

With a donated book I found in my room, I spent a lot of time in a lovely small room with Victorian scenes on the wallpaper. During one of their rounds, one young intern reminded me of a conversation he and I had on my first day. When he commented on how wild it was, his group leader called out his name and gave him a stern look. The intern immediately went quiet and changed his demeanor. His conversation brought to mind little snippets of memories of the day I was given that tiny pill, but not much more.

My admission into the VA Hospital was on a Monday, but Patrick was not allowed to visit until Wednesday. He was so torn up with blaming himself. He spent hours on the phone talking with my friend, Bobby. When we did meet, it took a lot to convince him, that what had happened was no one's fault. It happened because it was time. I told him a little of what I knew he would understand. I was much perturbed when he, again, made things all about himself.

The VA Hospital diagnosed me with severe PTSD (Post Traumatic Stress Disorder). My counselors said I would be on medication for life if I didn't do counseling; or take the medication for one year with counseling. Not one to shy away from fear, I requested therapy in what was regarded the fourth best

VA PTSD program in the country in Johnson City, TN. The counselor was booked for a couple of months before I could start therapy. I did find a PTSD therapist who was content to work with me until I got into the VA program. After I was home for a few days, I resumed my domestic chores, and Patrick went back to his den and TV. He said nothing more, because he felt things had gone back to normal. I never shared with Patrick what happened at the Oak tree out back.

There was a very large Oak tree about 100' up the hill from the house. It leaned slightly toward the creek, making it great for lounging against for shade on hot days. A day after I came home from the hospital, I still felt a fatigue that could not be slept away; and my soul ached from being battered with painful memories. I bent down and put my back against the tree and closed my eyes. Within a few moments, I felt the presence of a very gentle entity nearby and a soft humming of a song, much like a lullaby. The next thing I knew I was picked up like a baby in the arms of her mother and held close. The giant arms gently rocked me back and forth as I heard words whispered several times. In a few moments, I was laid back down against the Oak tree. When I opened my eyes, I was in a fetus position, still hearing the whispered words, "Know you are loved." They would become my signature.

So began my learning who I was and how to rebuild a new life. Over the next couple of months, my dreams revealed two more flashbacks that would awaken me and prevent me from sleeping. Adding to my problems, it took 28 days for my body to adjust to the medication, leaving me in an insomniac state for nearly a month. The sleep medication not working, I sat rocking for many hours in the dark. The memories of the forgotten garbage of my past traumas oozed out of the rusty pot of my broken mind. Sitting alone in the dark, I steadily rocked through hours of tears and frustrations, feeling as defenseless as a weak kitten. There was no controlling the tormenting memories of a lifetime of abuse passing before my mind – over and over again. During the year of counseling, I would mentally and emotionally crawl through the windows, between the cracks of doors, down the chimney, through all the hidden rooms, and eventually straight down the middle of Hell then out of it. Once out, I kept walking, sometimes crawling, but always moving forward. I went more into spirituality and relied a lot on Guidance to help me through the painful journey.

Five symptoms of PTSD are addictions to sex, drugs, alcohol, food, and over buying (hoarders); all being instant feel-good gratifications. The problem is, a PTSD victim will have an ego that is always in need of gratification. Sex is very addictive, and usually does not cost anything. I truly feel this is why there is so much rape. It is easy to find a prey, and the sex gratifies instantly. The individual doing the raping is not thinking of the victim. At the same time, the ego does not understand the why of the trauma, and not having control, is angry – an anger that needs to be fed anger. A lot of PTSD victims carry a silent hot core within themselves; ergo, a lot of misunderstood eruptions of violence. This is often why PTSD victims are reclusive, lest the act out or a flashback occurs.

To get my mind off things and retain some sort of normalcy, I attended the second course for Redirecting a Cooperative Classroom on October 7, 2003, and was certified. Sometimes, I wondered if I just got bored and needed something to occupy my brain. The course was longer than the first, with far more attendance. During this conference, I was stunned to find myself standing up at the mic after dinner. I said that I had not planned on attending, because of the flashback, even though I had registered, and explained why. Then I thanked everyone for their camaraderie. After I sat down, the president and facilitator, Kathryn Kvols, came over and hugged me. I cannot describe what that did to me, on many levels – never mind the elation.

One day, a year of counseling behind me, I looked out the kitchen window of the Dome. It occurred to me that I had been taking my anger out on a community that would not accept me. Most of the community was so backwards with their old-fashioned mountain beliefs, it would often frustrate me. I turned from the kitchen sink and looked to Patrick.

He said, "I know. We're moving."

Five years after we had moved, I spoke with a young lady at a book store in Morristown TN, a town about 45 minutes from Sneedville. When I gave her my name, she told me her mother was from Sneedville. I was surprised when she remembered my name. After a few minutes, she told me that her mother was angry with me. I knew why and said, "All the women are angry because I am no longer there to fight their battle."

"Yes," she quietly breathed.

"It would have been nice to have been told that rather than them always gossiping about me." I knew the women didn't have the courage to stand up for themselves, and if they had, their husbands or fathers would have beaten them down. I was glad for the move.

North Carolina

I had met someone in Spring Creek, North Carolina, through a mutual friend in Tennessee. After our decision to move out of Tennessee, Patrick and I went back for another visit to find property. Both of those relationships dissolved soon after our move – their decision. This again reminded me that we meet people in our lives for a purpose. That there are steps you need to take to go from one step to another to fulfill a need. When the need has been fulfilled, most often, the relationship dissolves.

I walk the Red Road with the belief that if you want a new life, you need to get rid of the old one. So, I methodically went through all of my possessions and tossed out or gave away everything relating to my life before the flashback, including my precious 1000-book library. Losing interest in weaving, I closed my Fiber Art Studio. My poor husband never liked changes. But, nevertheless, in 2005, we moved from Tennessee and went further back into the Appalachian Mountains of North Carolina on 12.3 acres of slanted mountain property with a killer view of five mountain. After the move, I finished therapy and was released from Johnson City to the Asheville VA Hospital. It took another 28 days to get off the PTSD medication.

Mountain ranges in winter.

While waiting for the double-wide house to be delivered and set up, I mowed the tall grass with our new riding lawn mower for the first time. I loved that 42", double-bladed Husqvarna. The 17-horse Kohler engine gave me a different sense of power. There was a patch of prickly vines I had not seen, and one of them got tossed up into the air and fell across my leg. The large thorns cut my shin deeply and was instantly painful. But I sat there on the mower laughing and crying at the same time like an insane person. I was thankful no one was driving on the road going alongside the property seeing me crying because of the pain, and laughing *because* I had felt the pain.

There was another 40-year suppressed flashback of my being on a beach with three men using a sheet to cover me head to waist. They had intentions of raping me. Over time, the fear in that scenario numbed me from the waist down. Since then, I had to be told when my legs were cut, because I held never felt it. That day, on my mower, I felt pain in my legs for the first time in nearly forty years. For the next six months, I could not leave my ankles crossed for more than a few moments without them hurting. My emotions began showing themselves, and I would often just sit silently, discerning them or walk away from people when I didn't know what else to do or say.

An electric pole went in first. A 16'x24' building was built that I thought would be my new studio. Eventually, a wall with a door was built to cut off an 8'x16' storage space to hold all of my extra belongings. But due to the lack of interest, my floor loom was sold, leaving the room empty. It was rented for a while to an artist who did photos on fabric. A lean-to was added to the back of the building for miscellaneous 'junk' in one opened side and my riding lawn mower in the other enclosed side.

The water well and wellhouse went in. You have never had good water, until you have drunk mountain water. It never ceased to amaze me how the utilities were placed on both the Tennessee and North Carolina properties without consulting either me or my husband. Yet, in both instances, everything was built around them. After the new house seat was dozed, our double-wide home was delivered and set up. The front of the house had an open view to the five mountain ranges. I built the 12'x20' porch with a 24'x4' ramp. The idea of a new life with a spacious home with six-inch walls elated me. For the first time in a very long time, I was happy.

PTSD victims will display their symptoms, if you know what to look for. They sit with their backs to the wall, vigilant of their surroundings. They often don't stay with one job, any one project, or with any one partner. They are easily bored, suspicious, always on alert. These traits will often make the victim reclusive. One never knows which two senses will trigger a flashback, or when. My husband was supportive at this time of my life, though he never fully understood me until the flashback when I explained to him the traits. I still remember him walking to the den with his arms waving up to the side, saying, "You were hurting and never even knew it." He rarely showed insights into our relationship, so that was a biggie. I relaxed even more.

While unpacking and settling into my new home, I found two pieces of documents I had not thrown out. One was about beekeeping based on Rudolph Steiner's biodynamic farming and the other on herbs. I intuitively set the beekeeping documents aside; not sure why bees caught my attention. Often though unaware of it, we know our future. The documents survived my move, and I am a firm believer in everything happening for a reason.

The other item I found and set aside was a box of index cards holding "patients" information. While in Michigan, I had been a Certified Herbalist and did clinical for a few years in the mid-80's while owning Cerelli's herb shop in Frederic, Michigan. The people who came were those for whom the doctors had no cure; yet, I failed no one. Each individual needed about three hours of conversation as I took down their medical information, diet regime, habits, etc. One woman was just a diet change, but had a profound cure. One gentleman was going to be placed in the hospital for hepatitis. Retested a couple days before hospital entry the test showed negative. His doctor asked, "Is it the same woman?" When he responded with a head nod, the doctor told him to never leave me. I also cured a baby with a particular new virus that had been putting other babies into the hospital. The father shared with his pediatrician what he had done based on my instructions. She shared it and kept many more babies out of the hospital. There were a couple physicians with whom I worked. I also taught herbology: the herbs, their history, category of ailment/healing, how to pronounce their Latin names and how to prepare them. Two nurses participated in a class.

Aerial view of the property

I loved creating. Soon after the house was delivered, a 12'x16' metal building was transported to the property and placed about 12' away from the house, with a water pump between. The building was for my tools, both woodworking and gardening. A fenced garden, filled with raised beds, was built alongside that metal building, with a small greenhouse built along the length of the building and a potting shed in the back of it. The large boulder at the corner cleverly helped level the garden. I later built an 80'x80' garden located about seventy feet in front of our home, with a six-foot fence to keep out the deer and rabbits. I loved working with Mother Earth and went about putting in the flowers I love, especially herbs. All of the gardens were organic.

We hired a local to build a roof over the porch and a set of steps on the other side of the ramp. The porch had to be leveled first, which was my first indication that my creative abilities had been impaired by the 1999 auto accident. I would learn that it would take six weeks to complete any creative projects. A 10'x16' porch and woodshop were added to the mountain side of the studio.

While I drank my coffee every morning, the five mountain ranges breathed as the morning mist rose with the sun; and I learned to breath with them. Their inhaled breaths had a way of reaching deep into and quieting my soul. While my emotional and mental aches and pains left with the exhaled breaths. The sounds of the creek running alongside our property momentarily washed away painful memories, as I slipped into an altered, meditative state.

At times when I heard the rill chuckling when the water washed over the stones, I wondered what the water had encountered in the rainfall before falling into the creek flowing from the mountain top. My porch was at 2200' altitude. To the left, during the winter through the bare trees, I could see Max Patch ... "next to the Tennessee state line in the Harmon Den area of Hot Springs, NC. At 4,629 feet this bald mountain offers 360-degree vistas of Mount Mitchell to the east and Great Smoky Mountains to the southwest. An abundance of ferns and grasses blanket the bald ...." *Wikipedia.

After years of practiced meditation, I found that if I sat long enough, I will automatically go into an altered state. Grasping only a little of my long-term memory, and the flashback taking my short-term memory; it was concluded that I would be vegetating on that porch for the rest of my life. I was still making holes into the wall of my long-term memory, but was not yet able to remember many things. I knew the knowledge was there, just didn't know where it was located or how to pull it through. To prevent stress, it was during these times, I would contemplate on my past and think about my life's journey to where I was and the why of the trip. Many times, when I go within, I would find myself in that space of light. It would be many more years before I would learn the purpose of that light.

Healing

Spring Creek Rock Building School

Soon after the major construction of our house and buildings, I went to the library in the old Meal Site building. It was located behind the old rock-house school that had been built in the 1880s, and schooled children until 1980's. I met several people while they were packing and moving library books the Meal Site to the new library in the old rock house building. After sharing my putting a whole library on the computer while working at a juvenile facility in Michigan, I was asked if I would do the same for the new Spring Creek library.

Quite a bit of my brain function healed in that library as I worked many, many hours organizing it, sorting through the books and entering them into the computer using the Dewey-decimal system. Our books were entered as such because we were told our library would one day become part of the county's main library. It never happened because Spring Creek was the "red-headed foster child" of the county. I love books. And as I got reacquainted with the computer again, I learned that, though the 1999 accident took away my anger, it left me with an interesting quandary.

Using Excel spreadsheet program, I would often confuse it with Lotus123; an older spreadsheet software I had learned a half-a-lifetime ago. One frustrating day I touched a key, and the letter just ran across the page; and continued to run across the page, even after I lifted up my finger. I thought something had gone awry with the computer. But when I touched a key again, nothing happened. When I tried typing again, the keyboard would not do what I wanted. I got up from the chair, went to the window and took deep breaths. Ten minutes later, I went back to the computer and had no further issues. The computer was never turned off.

Before the 1999 accident, my anger could prevent a car from starting; as my husband learned when we were having a bad argument. Getting out of the car, and moving 12' away was what it took for the motor to turn over. My mechanic in Sneedville didn't believe me, until after the fifth time Suzi was towed into his garage. He, again, couldn't find anything wrong with her. When I went to pick her up, he said, "She is ready, but let's go and talk." I vented my day to him. It seemed that after the 1999 accident, my frustrations or extreme stress would cause anything digital to go awry, including computers and cell phones. I often questioned that, until I drove to Virgina to lecture at a bee club. I was really stressed about driving home and arriving before dark. Using the GPS to get me home, the phone was plugged into the charger in the car; but died just as I pulled off the exit ramp. I recognized the area and knew my way home. All the other times the phone had charged in the car; but not that time. The only thing I could surmise, was that my hands were on the steering wheel of the car while the car was supposedly charging the phone. Even my husband would not allow me to touch his cell phone again when it had stopped working in my hand while we were arguing. He had to wait a couple minutes before he could use it.

The studio no longer rented, I went through the rest my things packed in the storage room, and placed some of the items into a large corner shelf unit I had just built in the studio. My sewing machines and accessories were in the studio; so, I created a table for it when I purchased a 6' Formica counter top and built sturdy legs and a shelf under it. I then went to converting the storage room into a small kitchen-like area. Paying $50 for a stainless-steel sink and a faucet, I plumbed them into a Formica countertop over a cabinet with side drawers and double doors underneath. A shorter matching cabinet was purchased, with double doors for the 2' square counter and placed on the other side of the door. I had cut the 2' off of an 8' Formica counter top. The remaining 6' was attached to a 5' counter that became the L-shape floor counter, with homemade shelves underneath. All matching countertops were $5 each and in new condition.

I built the shelves above the L-shaped counter. Quality drapery fabric, saved from many years before, was used for curtains for the overhead shelves and under the counters. Our son plumbed the water into the kitchen off the outside yard pump with an underground turnoff valve next to it. A small water heater was installed under the sink. I purchased a wall cabinet for over the sink. I am explaining in detail because I was proud. All-in-all, it was a job economically well done and it looked good.

It took three attempts to write the book, *My Journey to Peace with PTSD;* first time as a counselor; second time from a third-person perspective. The third time, I finally owned it, and wrote it from first-person view point. I held nothing back while a friend edited it for and with me. One needed to feel a thing to understand it, not just read about it; so, the book contains some graphic scenarios. It was published January 2007, by my Peace Publishers company. I first sold quite a few on Amazon then other companies took over the sales before it went global. What surprised and pleased me was that all the therapists and counselors I heard from said they had learned something from the book. Soon after publication, someone asked me a question to which I had carried the answer for sixty years. I had to go to the book to get the answer, and that showed me how much I had healed from writing it.

July 2007, I had a heart attack and a triple-bypass surgery; an issue created from the medication Avandia, a diabetic drug. When I mentioned this to my doctor, she told me it was not true. Three months after my heart surgery, Avandia was taken off the market because it caused heart issues. By October, I was walking the hills with a small backpack during a 3-day herbal workshop. During 2007, I did a couple of book signings and traveled to Florida for a weekend conference on Sexual Assault.

Beekeeping

In 2009, I saw a poster in our post office about a bee school being held in Asheville, NC, and signed up. I wanted to do something different and was not afraid of bees. Besides, I wanted my own honey. I also felt the bees could take care of themselves if I got caught up into something else, which was normal for me. Within a couple of years, the honeybees would become my passion and purpose. Never have I encountered such an animal that could take from the plants and trees as they did and create healing powers. The bees give all they have and ask for nothing in return except to be left alone to do their thing.

I would learn that honey can cure wounds. Bee pollen alone can sustain a human being for six months. Propolis cures cancer and MRSA. Bee Air can make lung tumors disappear in a matter of weeks. But what would take me many more years to learn is the sound of the honeybee buzz would help me with my PTSD symptoms and get me back out into the world. The bees changed my life in the most unexpected and unimaginable ways by being at my side every step of my major growths and healings. My life kept changing as I changed with it.

Past memories, forgotten since 1999, slipped back into my brain through the memory holes. Or I was able to mentally grab hold of it and pull it through. The hormones and chemicals in my brain related to PTSD normalized as best they could. Every time I worked a hive; I healed from emotional scars and past traumas. The torments of my abusive childhood that took me through troubled teen years and the multiple rapes in the military no longer governed my life. They had easily slipped into a special place in my brain where I could see them.

Often the bees humming brought up good thoughts or memories. A bee's hum resonates at the key of C – which is my key – that vibrates about 263 Hertz. A bee's hive needs to resonate about 195 to 250 Hertz for optimal health. The colony can vibrate at about 600 Hertz or more before and during a swarm. This reminded me of my drumming lessons. A djembe beat resonates at about 400 Hertz. When I first started taking djembe instructions, the instructor had me try beating the heartbeat on the drum – ba bump, ba bump. I couldn't do it. After several attempts, I got upset, excused myself and left. I didn't remember the drive home.

That night I dreamt of lying in a flat-bottomed boat on very calm water. Within a few moments, a dark shadow swam toward the boat, reached in a hand and stroked me. The specter swam away, only to be followed by another that also reached in and briefly stroked me. The strokes were not felt physically, but by my emotional heart. I never felt threatened. I just laid there while five more specters swam to the boat and stroked me. I awoke soon after the last apparition swam away. When I opened my eyes, I laid in bed and felt a warm sensation of relief wash over me. I intuitively knew that the seven ghostly beings were the essences of my lost babies; telling me that it was okay, and that I was loved. My heart lightened as I arose from my bed with a smile. I went back to the djembe class and joyfully thumped out the heartbeat.

Each step on my healing journey taught me a little bit more about myself; each revelation rendering a different part of me. I gradually came out from under the black cloak where I had buried myself. The mirror slowly reflected who I had always wanted to be, but never saw. I was generous; a listener; gentle with people; embraced them and told them they were loved. It was surprising to see how many men cry when I had hugged them after they shared the loss of their partner. Caretakers do not always have their needs met while tending their loved ones during illnesses. As I saw more of my reflected self, I was delighted to see that I could actually learn to love myself, albeit slowly.

My first apiary

I had a large ambition of becoming a very good beekeeper. In 2009, I won my first colony at the Asheville Bee School and bought another colony to create my first apiary. I didn't have to think long or hard where to locate it. I could look out my window and see them in the orchard about 100' from the back of the house. A couple of years later, the apiary grew to eight hives and were moved to an enclosed area behind the healing room. After an enclosed porch and a new woodshop was built that contained the many tools that made men drool, I made a lot of my own bee equipment and stored them underneath the porch section. Mr. Wagner, my high school woodshop teacher, often popped into my mind whenever I worked in my woodshop. He always reminded me of the toy-maker in the Pinocchio movie.

Soon after getting my colonies, I joined our local bee club and began talking with local beekeepers, especially one old-timer named Sherm. He taught me the basics and the beginnings of respecting the honeybee. He also told me to stop feeding the bees after November – which I did. Soon after I had stopped feeding, a bee came to my large kitchen window while I was doing dishes. She moved up, down, and turned around; and did it twice more. I silently asked what she wanted. "We are hungry," came the mental response. It didn't occur to me to wonder at my hearing the bee.

I immediately dried my hands, went to the utility room and made a gallon of sugar feed. I fed them for another month. In the spring, I spotted the round dark spots on the outside of their hives. Research indicated that sugar feed had no nutrients and caused the bees to develop Nosema; a disease that caused the diarrhea spots outside the hive. The winter diarrhea went away after they got nutrient-rich nectar with lactobacillus in the spring. After that, I listened to my bees and became a no-treatment beekeeper. I was talked about and almost ostracized from the bee club while members made fun of me. No problem. I was actually sad for the other beekeepers. They were blinded by money, and still lost a lot of bees.

As I aged, I would research what was going on in my body, and took the high-quality supplement to help it or balance out what medication was destroying. The more I researched, the more curious I became, until I took a course in nutrition. In December 2009, I received my Certification as a Nutritional Consultant from the Global college of Natural Medicine.

Getting serious about beekeeping, In May 2010, I took a course on Born and Bred in North Carolina, a Queen Rearing Workshop sponsored by the North Carolina Cooperative Extension. In June of that same year, I became a Certified Beekeeper, sponsored by the NC Agricultural Extension Service and the NC State Beekeepers Association. April 2011, I received my certification as Master Herbalist from the Global College of Natural Medicine. In April 2010, I signed up for the International Apitherapy Course, Levels I, II, & III taught by Dr. Stephan Stangaciu from Romania, a world-wide Apitherapy instructor. I finished the course with a thesis on propolis and was certified in 2015.

To date, though Apitherapy is practiced by some acupuncturists and holistic healers, it is not recognized by the American Medical Association. In recent years, the FDA has approved Manuka honey; but I won't use it. Honey contains anti-bacterial, anti-viral, anti-fungal, and anti-microbial properties. FDA uses Gamma^2 rays to destroy the anti-microbial properties of Manuka honey. I use local, organic honey for healing purposes and in my food regime. It is proposed that the bacterial (botulinum) microbes in honey is the reason you don't feed it to infants less than two years old. But my ancestors have used honey in infants' feeding bottles for as long as I can remember. Honey nourishes and heals.

The gardens and land around the house were planted with bee plants. Two Bee-Bee trees were planted in the large fenced garden and bloomed during the July and August dearth. There were 24 hives in three apiaries by 2014, with my doing a small number of "studies" – if you can call them that – in the main apiary. Respect was given to my bees before I approached their hives then placed my hand on top of the hive to send love and good thoughts.

Stress was always released as the honeybees took me into their world and embraced me while I learned apitherapy. I loved to learn, just so I could teach. I transformed my "studio" into a healing room with a table made to hold a covered, single foam mattress. Bee Venom Therapy was used as I taught people how to sting for Lyme Disease and other ailments.

---

[2] https://www.sciencedirect.com/science/article/pii/S2772275922000053

Bored and with time on my hands, I researched for six months to create a lotion formula using bee products. I finally came up with one and accidently learned how to keep the oils and other liquids from separating. My Vita Mix got really hot when in use, and I found that the heat and speed was what emulsified the ingredients. This experiment compelled me to take a lab course at our local college. I was certified in October 2012, in Basic Lab Skills from Asheville-Buncombe Technical Community College. I knew the woman who was president of the Good Manufacturing Product (GMP) division and gave her a small jar of my lotion. She was greatly impressed by the fact that a couple of years later, it still had not separated. The lab course had served me well when, several years later, it helped me to understand while I created my own Lacto-water for my bees. The Lacto-water was a way of giving my bees the lactobacilli the Roundup prays was killing in the hive and in the bees.

The newly built kitchen in the healing room was transformed into my mini-lab with two microscopes, a mini centrifuge, a lot of instruments and accessories, a few petri dishes, and other tools. I picked up every little thing I could to add to my lab. When Patrick was in the hospital ER, the doctor brought in a cloth-covered set of tools. When she opened them up, I saw what they were. I had asked what she planned on doing with them when she was done with her exam. When she said they tossed them, I asked if I could have them and explained why. She left the room and came back with a larger set. When she was done, she handed me the rolled-up cloth of tools. I told her I loved her. Goodness, but I was excited and felt blessed.

Picture of a bee's wing

In my lab, I looked at a bee's wing up closely, and became more fascinated with the world of science. One of my microscopes was able to take pictures of whatever was on the slide. I used a centrifuge to separate my honey to find pollen, then used a microscope and a pollen book to see if I could identify the pollen. I learned this process while visiting a pollen specialist at the University of Entomology in Turin, Italy, during the Terre Madre Festival in 2010. A lot of my time was spent in my lab.

PART VII
Living the Life

Terre Madre International Festival

In the summer of 2010, I walked into the office of my Agricultural Extension Agent and found David Kendal intensely looking at a piece of paper. When he looked up at me, he asked if I would like to go to Italy? Thinking he was kidding, I said, "Sure." To my surprise and glee, I was chosen to be one of eight delegates from Slow Food International of Asheville District to attend the Terra Madre Festival in Turin, Italy, held October 21-25. My disposition usually allowed me to accept and deal with anything and everything that came along. But this was international, and it was hard to contain my excitement.

A fundraiser was held at our local Spring Creek Sunswept Farms, where a well-known chef from Asheville prepared a large dinner cooked on open coals. The $35 paid by each of the 200 people from three counties was used to pay for each delegate's round-trip flight to Turin. The delegates paid for everything else beyond the plane tickets. My contribution to the meal was my homemade cannoli – a lot of them. I am an excellent cook.

Rosa and Clara

I emailed the Italian Federation of Beekeepers, who forwarded the email to Pietro Viazzo, their past president and 30-year board member. Pietro responded to me immediately, and plans were made for him to meet the three of us at our apartment in Turin (Torino). We met Pietro's sister, Rosa, and her good friend Clara, our interpreter. Rosa and I still stay in touch.

Several weeks before departure, I researched apartments for the three of us women that was easily accessed by public transportation and close to the venue. The apartment had one queen bed, which Julie and Vanessa shared; I took the cot. The unfamiliar gas stove forced us to eat out most of the time, though we did learn to boil water for tea. Terre Madre offered an excellent free lunch every day of the festival, so we did have at least one good meal a day. We also had a clothes washer/dryer combo from Hell, which Vanessa used for one load of laundry the day before she left. At the end of eight hours of operation, she stopped the machine, packed the wet clothes, and took them to France with her.

Pietro and Rosa shared the driving, while we three, and sometimes, Julie, toured in and around Turin. In truth. My eyes were closed a lot while we drove through downtown Turin. Though nearly all drivers displayed some sort of courtesies by honking their car horns before jumping into traffic, their kind of road courtesies did nothing for my stress level.

Activities

Entertainment was done in one building near the stage with natives from different countries singing and dancing while attired in their native dress. The same building also held international vending, with wares on display on the middle of the floor and along one wall. The ambience in the air held joyful camaraderie with everyone smiling and laughing. Even children were dancing and laughing while their parents shopped. Something was always happening.

African Delegates   Russian Delegates

People from around the world attended the festival, many wearing their traditional dress. I had never before attended such an affair, and often wondered what I had done to be blessed at age 67. And to think, two years before, all I wanted was a of couple of hives for honey.

The food part of the festival was the Salone Del Gusto. Walking down the middle of the main hall of the very large building was so crowded, it got downright personal as bodies rubbed. I couldn't slap away the hands because I could not discern which hand had patted my butt. I held the largest organic red pepper I had ever seen. I tasted wine from many countries. Samples of different kinds of meats and cheeses from many European countries were abundantly and beautifully displayed.

My biggest joys were meeting people in the International Beekeepers room. I maintained some of their contacts for a while after I left Italy. International travelers taught me how they brought large jars of honey in their checked luggage. The International Honey bar gave me the opportunity to taste honey from around the world. Cabbage honey from Hungary tasted like how a wet dog smells, and my face expressed my displeasure. The taste was immediately cut by the aromatic honey from the perfumed white flowers of the Corsican Plantes des Maquis, located on Corsica Island off the coast of France. Because of the one and only type of bee, no other kinds of bees were allowed on that island.

Yumiko Fugiwara, Japan

I met Yumiko Fugiwara from Japan at the International Honey Tasting Bar and kept her contact. In December, 2019, Yumiko invited me to Japan to join their 1st Annual Honeybee Conference, which I did attend.

Honey Tasting Class

The Honey Tasting Class showed how the Italians treat honey like wine. There is a science in detecting the aroma, taste, grade, texture, color, etc., to every type of honey on the earth. And if honey does not contain pollen, it likely has been filtered to prevent detecting the honey's source of origin.

Carl Chesick, Executive Director of the Center for Honeybee Research, appointed me the post of Ambassador a few days prior to my leaving for Turin. I took it to heart. When I first introduced myself, the people were "Honored to meet someone in that capacity." I confess to feeling honored myself, and feeling a bit awkward. I came from a family of hillbillies of Tennessee Mountains and had not been taught social graces beyond thank you and please. The ambassador position put me into a whole new world as I joyfully grew into its grace that changed my military language. Over the next few years, it would also change me. The position gave me the opportunity to experience places, people, and conversations I would never have had otherwise. My white hair also did its magic to give the notion that I had wisdom. The more I grew into the role, the quieter I became. It no longer seemed necessary to verbalize my thoughts. I learned to respond only when asked because only until then will someone usually be receptive to a response. My asking permission does the same thing.

I felt out of place at first, yet curiously found my place as I met with other beekeepers from around the world. Pietro arranged a tour with a local beekeeper and a tour at a local organic cattle farm for me and Julie. The farmer's barn had about ten stalls. Each stall containing a single cow ranging from a very young calf in the first stall with each stall to the right holding an older, larger cow. Each of the ten stalls had their own door to an outside individual pen, where the cows were let out each day for about an hour. The cows were fed organic food in individual troughs in front of their stalls. The farmer was proud of his organic cows. Though intrigued, I wasn't sure what to think of the whole operation.

Rosa took me and Julie to Pietro's for Sunday dinner where we met his son, Piotra, and his wife. Pietro's wife, Maria Therese cooked us a large, delicious luncheon. A couple days before we were to leave, Clara, our interpreter, took me to Turin's oldest, 200-year-old restaurant, where we dined on Caviar hors d'oeuvres and pasta for lunch. I must have ingested a parasite because I could not void my bowels and had gained ten pounds before I left Italy.

Dinner in our honor

The day before we flew out, Clara arranged with her friend to close her restaurant and host we three delegates for a dinner, along with some of their close friends. I felt honored to be treated so well by new friends. I learned on my visit the following year that Rosa and Clara's friendship had ended. Rosa would not tell me what had happened, but assured me it was okay.

Meeting people on an international scale gave me a whole new perspective of human nature. Even though we may have two legs, two arms, and a torso, the minds of people are so different because of cultures, life-styles and basic belief tenets. When I came back, I gave a Power Point of my trip and saw that I was the one who actually made use of the trip. I brought back connections that would take me back to Italy and other places in the world. Not even my two companions commented on my Power Point. David said I was the only one who brought anything back and used the experience to advance myself in the beekeeping world. And goodness, did I! I will always be grateful for David for extending such a fantastic opportunity to me. I firmly believe that Guidance always opens the doors when we are ready and on the right path.

I don't know what Vanessa did during her time in Italy. Most of the time, we three delegates did our own thing. I never saw the other five delegates.

Travels from 2011 through 2013

55-gallon drums.

I went back to Italy a couple more times and interviewed another beekeeper, a professor at the University of Entomology and people in two bee labs. Another visit found me at CONAPI, National Beekeepers Consortium – biodiversity farmers. CONAPI collects about 10,000 gallons of honey from beekeepers from all over Italy and bottles the honey under the CONAPI label.

I went back to Italy and stayed with Rosa. During each of my visits, our "women's luncheon" was held in private rooms in different cafés with the number of women growing to about fourteen. In Italy, bars are known as cafes, and businesses serving alcohol are called saloons. I found it curious how diverse Italy was with their acceptance of different cultures, languages, foods…. Exploring their exquisite, enormously large, marble statues and art throughout the city reminded me of how little diversity there is in USA's outdoor art. Rosa's Catholic church, built in the 1500's, reminded me of how young America is. Often little things intrigue me; like the single path in the church's stone floor that led to the pulpit, worn by 1500 years of people walking to the pulpit for the sacraments during services.

What annoyed me was not being able to find a receptacle adapter for my phone in any office or computer store. But I did find one at what we would call a flea market; the Italians call a "ghetto." Their homeless people are called gypsies. The "ghetto" district was a clean, asphalt-paved space with vendors displaying their wares on blankets or on tables. I didn't see any tents, but was told they had housing in the same area. I smiled at watching a mother and daughter gleefully playing, until someone passed by them. They immediately transformed their faces into sad, pathetic people. I was not comfortable with their ease of transformation and was glad to leave the gypsies.

During my stay, I had the occasion of doing one load of laundry in Rosa's apartment. She lives on the fourth floor of an apartment building with a concierge where the tenants own their own apartments. Rather than using her dryer, I had asked if it was possible to hang my clothes outdoors. We went out a narrow door from her tiny kitchen onto her small 4'x8' patio. The "clothes line" was attached to her patio railing and suspended out about two feet. It consisted of eight lines between two metal bars spaced about three feet apart, angled upward. The six lines were about three inches apart. Afraid of heights, I warily stretched out to the last line and hung my underwear, and worked my way toward the patio rail. Dropping her cleaning rag, I had asked what happened if I dropped anything down to the enclosed ground below. I was told I would have to buy new, as the space below was inaccessible. She dismissed the rag, and I didn't do any more laundry.

My travels as Ambassador helped me to do a great deal of research while writing the Center's monthly magazine. It eventually turned into a quarterly magazine when it became too much for me to create every month. While spending about 30 hours a week on the Center's newsletter, I was also writing a newsletter for my own website – the non-profit BEe Healing Guild Org. Both newsletters were different. I also started doing a little research in my bee yards, not so much in scientific research in my lab, but more by observing the bees' behaviors, listening to them and doing small experiments.

<u>Senegal, Africa, 2011</u>

When I got back from Italy in 2010, I was contacted by a beekeeper names Ousmane in Dakar, Senegal, Africa, through an interpreter. We texted for a few months before making plans for my visit to Senegal in 2011 after my Italy visit. When I got to Senegal, I met our interpreter, Jean Chekh Ndiaye, and his brother Andre Waly Ndiaye. I stayed in Dakar with Ousmane's daughter. Though I was monetarily generous to the family, I was not always treated with respect. Ousmane's nephew lived upstairs and was our interpreter while I stayed with her. Jean and Andre did most of the interpreting while we traveled; and I got to know the two brothers.

Side view of a fishing complex administration building.

We traveled for many days, visiting many places. One trip included a visit to a coastal fishing village and market that included an administration building, which is about 36' wide and about 70' long. While touring the building, Ousmane pointed out the dark spots on the inside walls and said they were honey. "No," I corrected him. "They spots are bee poop," I closed my eyes and listened to the massive sounds coming from the ceiling. My imagination ran wild wondering about the number of colonies that were up there and how much honey there was.

Front view of administration building on fishing complex, facing the ocean.

After introductions were made, the director asked if the bees in the roof could be removed. I explained the removal process and spraying a toxic paint after the bees and combs were removed. Then I further explained that the bees would come back, because in the heat, the toxic odor would evaporate, and the bees would return. They had to close off the bees' entrance in the eaves of the roof. Pointing to a honeybee coming through the open window and another leaving, I told him that he was already cohabitating with the bees. He was not happy at the idea of forever coming into the building every morning and someone shoveling the three to five inches of dead bees off the floor along the wall. I still kept thinking of the enormous amount of filled honeycombs under the building's roof.

I was escorted to a medicine woman's home a short distance away on the same compound. She explained that three medicine men had spent three days in a building filled with bees on the same compound. When the men came out in the morning of the third day, they said the bees had communicated that bad things would happen if the bees were harmed. The bees stayed. When we came out of the medicine woman's house, I gave her a hug, and she eagerly hugged me back. I was told it was unusual for her; but I understood why.

Women cleaning fish and drying them on racks under a roof

The fishing village showed me the African way of life of those living near the ocean. A family can spend their whole life fishing, cleaning, drying, selling/trading their fish on a daily basis; and not move beyond several hundred feet from the ocean's edge. Their only travel would to buy essentials in the nearby village.

Most forms of private transportation

A mule and cart are a common type of conveyance for transporting large items to the market and getting around. I had asked to ride in one for the experience, but didn't take another after watching the driver beat the horse. I saw many signs of horse/mule neglect and abuse.

Sitting around the campfire

I wasn't sure if it was a test for a female elder, but in that one day we walked for miles from breakfast until late in the evening. At dusk time, we met with the village chief. I gratefully sat down with him and his family. Later when the stars were out, we met with another village chief and his family. I declined to sit, because I knew that if I had, I would need help in getting up. After that last visit, I was escorted to a hotel, and the men went elsewhere; but were back early the next morning.

I don't know how many villages we had visited, but Africa fascinated me. I thought of my own lifestyle in my youth and adulthood, and wondered if I could live the way Africans did. Then, I would remember my aunt's small farm and knew we had lived a similar life, but in subtle, different ways. I, too, was raised poor, with no shoes in summer. We wore donated clothes that went from the largest to the smallest until they eventually went to either quilts or rags. Our family received food from the government or donations; Christmas gifts came off the Salvation Army truck, etc. That was why Africa felt somewhat familiar. I never saw the poor – just the people. They were friendly, but curious and cautious.

What was annoying was that no matter how you traveled, either by bus or car, the locals would hawk (sell) their wares in loud voices through the window or actually get on the bus. But what bothered me the most were the very small young boys in dirty, torn clothing, begging for money. I was told it was a way for them to learn the Quran while begging/working for a Muslim holy man. One lad was verbally aggressive when I closed the car window and turned my back on him. I had once made the mistake of giving someone a coin and was nearly mobbed. Didn't do that again.

Lady dressed in traditional African dress with Cissy.

Open market

Shopping was fun in the common outdoor markets. Often, there were many, many tents or makeshift buildings touching each other at the road's edge, with just enough room for a vehicle between the road and tent. The closeness of the stores made me think of our flea markets here in the States. Meats were cut in an open-air market under a roof.

Monkeys everywhere had the right-of-way, and they knew it. If you didn't watch your food when you put it down, it and the monkey would often quickly disappear. After a while, you came to understand they were the blurs in your vision.

During my visit, everyone used my phone to save their credits (paid time on a cell phone), and I carried no CFAs (Senegal currency) with me. I finally ran out of credits on my phone, and my AAA debit card didn't work. I had to go to the American Embassy to wire my husband to send me money. Jean saw my situation and, without my asking, took $40 from his meager savings to tie me over until I got my wire. He did not ask for it back. It is very hard for me to ask for help. But I did not forget his generosity. That gift deeply endeared me to him.

Toulouse, France, October, 2011

Dr. John Kefuss and Lady

Not sure how I found him, but Dr. John Kefuss, Zoologist in Toulouse, France, showed up on my radar. After connecting with him, I made arrangements to visit him. His house in Toulouse is about ten minutes from the airport. As you can see in the photo, I didn't do much with my hair while traveling. We went grocery shopping on the way home from the airport, and John bought simple things to fix for our meals. And the rule was, everything had to be eaten until it was gone. That proved to be difficult for me. I was raised with leftovers and avoided them as much as possible as an adult, leaving Patrick with our leftovers.

Driving through the gated walls up to his house, I saw John's enclosed front wild-looking yard. He and his wife both love nature and live close to it, as much as possible, and prefer the yard's wild look. His wife, Josette, a mushroom aficionado, was at a mushroom conference. Architecture often fascinates me because it gives me a sense of the culture of those whom I visit, and John's house did not disappoint me. The woodwork was very dark due to its age. The windows were narrow, about eight feet tall, with cobwebs in the bottom corners. I said nothing about the cobwebs. It wasn't for me to criticize how others keep their home. Have I mentioned that I despise dusting anything? The cobwebs were okay with me. The bathroom was downstairs, and the large upstairs bedroom with three beds was where I had slept. John prepared dinner and cleaned up afterwards.

He talked about driving out into the country the next day where he kept his many of his 500 hives. Early the next morning, we drove about two hours into the country. John and I were too busy talking for me to remember to take pictures of the countryside. Our conversations always flowed easily.

House to the left, barn to the right

When we arrived at the 200-year-old farm house. John explained that when it was built, it was felt the animals were part of the family, since they sustained the humans with milk, eggs, meat, etc. So, the barn that housed the animals was accessed through a kitchen door. The house was sparse in furnishings and appliances – and I do mean sparse. The kitchen had a sink and a table, with the only two chairs in the entire house. A few shelves were along one wall in the kitchen. His "office" was in the back of the house. Even mostly empty, the house had good energy.

During dinner, John asked why I had not mentioned his cobwebs in the corners of the windows. I told him it was not something I would do, and that it was his house. If he was pleased with them, I was tickled. He suggested I go and look at the cobwebs. When I got to the window, he asked me what I saw. I told him insects, dust … He said, "They are my fly catchers."

I looked again and understood when I saw the flies. "Clever!" I stated. He then explained that he allowed the spiders to build the cobwebs all year-round, then cleaned them up in the spring. He was right about there not being anything flying and the place being clean of dust. Air movement caused the dust to move around and be caught by the cobwebs. Truly clever! But my thoughts went to the spiders and were there that many.

John pitching my bed

We went through the door to the right of the kitchen entrance that led to the barn and the loft. Turning left, we walked around and up the cement steps with no railing that ascended up to the loft. John immediately grabbed the pitchfork and asked how I liked my bed. I thought he was joking, until he started pitching the hay. His bed was on the other side of the loft.

Lady pitching her pillow

The one thing that stayed on my mind was the very large opening to the outside between our sleeping spaces. John said it was used to bring in hay bales, but it was also used by night owls dining on their preys – pointing to the small bones next to the back wall. He then handed me the pitchfork, and I finished my bed with a "pitched" pillow. He placed a sheet over the hay, then placed the blanket on top. Looking at the bed with satisfaction, John said, "You will sleep like a baby." He was right. I didn't remember a thing after my head hit the hay, so to speak.

At the end of the cement steps, a shovel stood alongside a door to the outside. I will share that this shovel and I became intimate partners for what I termed the "shovel dance." One walks about 200 feet to the back of the property to a large square open space beyond the bushes. You dug in your shovel; moved the dirt to one side; did your voiding business; then covered your business with the dirt that had been shoved to the side.

Years later, I would wonder if holding "my business" isn't what caused my constipation while traveling. There were unusual cultural practices, like using your fingers in Africa instead of toilet paper. When one was done with the shovel dance, the shovel was put back alongside the door inside the barn. I smiled every time I danced with the shovel – so nostalgic. Baths were taken in a 55-gallon barrel. I took sponge baths because even though there was a step to help me over the barrel's edge, there was nothing inside the barrel to help me out of it. Short legs, don't you know!

French beekeeper

Whenever John and I were still, we exchanged personal experiences as we drove through the countryside touring and visiting people. We didn't go to any touristy sites, which was okay with me. We visited his neighbor and his cattle. We also visited another commercial beekeeper neighbor who also repaired antique clocks. He had the largest honey extractor I had ever seen.

Lady working on frames

John showed me his lab in another building that held only a chair and a table with a microscope. He would artificially inseminate his queens and ship them all over the world. I stayed with John for two days and two nights in the country, sometimes helping him with his bee equipment. I did work on his frames to ready them for the boiling vat when he took them back to the bee house in Toulouse.

Wax Foundation Melter

When we got back to Toulouse, we went to his workshop located not far from his house. It was where he kept his machinery, and where he and his son made their own bee equipment. I was shown how to melt the wax foundation onto the vertical wires in the frames using a machine that heated the wires. I was not experienced and pretty much made a mess of a few frames. During the tour of the workshop, John taught me ways to clean the equipment and how other bee equipment was made. He had an incinerator in his shop's yard where he burned old wax and broken wooden pieces.

Visiting China often, John was learning the Chinese language while showing the beekeepers how to artificially inseminate their honeybee queens. It seems the Chinese had sprayed so many chemicals on their crops, they nearly decimated their entire honeybee population. Actually, John can speak six languages. He shared about his partner in Chile where they had about 4,000 hives, from where they also shipped queens around the world.

Me and Josette

John shared that when he met Josette at a conference in the United States, he spoke English; she spoke French. They both knew Spanish, and that was how they communicated until John learned French. When they married, he followed her to France and stayed.

When we arrived back at the house in Toulouse, Josette, reprimanded us for leaving behind the leftover food that she had to eat. After dinner, I showered and packed for my morning flight back to the States. After putting on my pajamas, I joined John in his office where he showed me his thirty years of beekeeping journals. They were not small books, but encyclopedia size, all full, and all on a single shelf built on three walls within his reach. During our casual sharing at his computer, he emailed several documents on the *Varroa destructor*. John has had many international students visiting him through many years of teaching. But I got the impression I was his last student. We hugged at the airport and kept in touch for many years.

Senegal, Africa, May and October, 2013

Ousmane spent several days trying to impress me during my previous visit. I knew he wanted a "sugar mama," but I was not having any part of it. I stated there was nothing I could do for him, and politely said so when he handed me a project list of $100,000. The plan was to visit Ousmane again, but during a WhatsApp call two weeks prior to the May, 2013, visit, I had asked Ousmane if he wanted me to teach him beekeeping. He shook his head no. His nephew translated and added that we elders had to resolve our issues. I had bought his nephew a laptop, and knew he was looking for what else he could garner out of me. I explained it was not my issue, and that I was not in a position to pay for their projects. I wished Ousmane well and thanked his nephew. Neither were happy. I knew they didn't want me – they wanted money.

During the next two trips that year, I stayed with Jean and his family. I slept with Cissy while Jean slept in the living room on the floor mat with the children. In a one-bedroom apartment, it is common for family members to sleep with one another on the same mattress. In Jean's and Cissy's home, I offered to help clean the rice that was cooked in the morning and served in a very large oval platter at the mid-afternoon and evening meals. Variations of fried fish, sometimes goat or beef, with some vegetables and a peanut sauce, are served over the rice. Everyone uses individual spoons to eat from the same oval platter. And when I say everyone, this includes visitors and extra family members. A couple can start out as newlyweds and before the end of first anniversary and money allows, there is a baby, a sibling, or a family member living with them. Eventually, it becomes a noisy happy crowd in one household.

Me cleaning rice for cooking

Ironing with a coal ember

Africa life appears harsh. But once there and living it, you adapt – and things strange become familiar. In the photo of the clothes iron to the left, the iron is heated with hot embers placed in the chamber above the bottom plate. Therese is ironing on a blanket on the table. Sometimes she places a blanket on the floor and irons while sitting with her legs stretched out in front of her. Laundry is done one day a week by hand without a scrubbing board and hung out on lines on the building's roof top. If it's rainning, laundry is hung in the kitchen area.

Lady sitting in the back

Jean's daughter, Madeleine, asked if I would speak to her 4th-grade class. Andre came as my translator; but it wasn't really necessary, since the students had learned English. So, Andre and I stood up there, as I shared a little of my life, and why I was in Dakar. During the Q&A, someone had asked my age. I thought I would impress them with my prowess in math, so I held up both hands for each ten years of my age. When I got to sixty, I lost count and turned to Andre and asked how many it was. The teacher laughed when Andre reminded me. I then held up another ten fingers to indicate seventy. As if on cue, the whole class of students sat down in their seats. I turned to Andre and asked what I had said. He told me that Senegalese people my age were not as active nor as agile as I was. Having seen the locals, I found he was correct.

Not familiar with my surroundings, I was not always that conscious of what was going on around me, making me grateful for Andre and Jean. After that, I made an effort to be more aware. When I traveled, it was with one foot in this reality and the other in the spirit world, because I did not know who or what I would encounter. I trusted Guidance that much.

Lady with grandchildren – Little Lady, Germaine and Madeleine

It seemed I never sat down without a child coming into my lap. Senegal families are large, and giving. At about two years old, children are taught to share by giving them a piece of candy to suck on, then taking it away and sharing it with another family member. It seems to work. There was an occasion when I had been introduced to a young child eating bread and was offered a broken piece. I took it and thanked him.

Unpainted public bus

Traveling was an adventure in and of itself. What was most enjoyable were the public transportation buses painted in psychedelic colors with no glass pane in the windows. One walked on top of 100-pound bags of grain on the floor to get to their seat. Even on the more modern buses, a man hanging onto the outside of the back door was seen swinging on the door when the bus was moving. He was always readily available to help people toss their bags of grain, luggage, or whatever, on top of the bus.

The city was always loud with honking noises, constant crowding, hawkers and beggars of all ages; always moving outside the bus window. People were friendly; but real discussions were rare. One significant memory still haunts me. During a long bus ride, I watched a woman with a cloth bundle in her lap staring out the window with a face holding disillusionment and hopelessness. I never saw her head move from looking out the window. It brought to mind of my sitting on my front porch after temporarily losing both long-term and short-term memories, thinking I was going to be sitting there for the rest of my life.

Square Plots of Dried Sea Salt

Images stay with me, as I remember the square plots of white 'stuff' on the desert floor alongside man-made channels of water coming from the sea. When I asked, Jean explained that after the square plots are dug out, a heavy fiber is laid down into the square. Sea water is then poured on the fiber in the square and allowed to dry. Water is continually added, until there are about six inches of dried salt. Heavy equipment then removes the salt and piles it to the side. The salt is sold and transported to a business that packages and ships it as mineral or sea salt. I had to laugh when I thought of paying $7 for the "mineral salt" that may actually be from one of those plots.

Nemending, Senegal, Africa

Leone Ndiaye with his coiled beehive

While in Dakar, Jean, Andre and I traveled to Nemending to meet their uncle Leone, a medicine man and true bushman. What impressed me was his going out into the bush at midnight and hunting with his Russian rifle, to which he referred his second wife. He often would come back with a wild boar. Now, I am here to tell you that when you are in the bush after sundown, you cannot see your hand in front of your face; and there didn't seem to be any stars at night. For him to come back with a boar at 3 AM was more than impressive.

A straw blind with two holes for the gun.

Leone was the caretaker of a 3,000-acre mango grove orchard. He would sometimes sit in his makeshift blind made from straw to kill the monkeys that were in the mango trees – his method of taking care of tree pests.

Water well   Women grinding millet

Life in the bush is not easy. A water well is used to draw water for drinking, laundry, cooking, bathing – everything. As for cooking, the women dropped a very large pestle in a large wooden mortar bow and ground the millet into flour for meals. If you listened closely, you could hear a rhythm, as the two women rocked back and forth, taking turns dropping the pestle on the millet. After I came home, I could often hear this rhythm while meditating at home.

During my second day, Leone leaned in very close to Jean, and told him to translate a dream he had two years before my arrival. It was of a star coming down to the village saying that a white woman was going to come, and that they had to love her as their own. I will confess that when I and Leone locked eyes for the first time, there was a sense of familiarity I had not had with anyone else in Africa, except for maybe Andre. Leone was concerned about his lack of money, about how he was going to feed the three of us. I knew of their poverty and had given Jean the equivalent of $40 for our two-day stay.

This was equivalent to a week or two of pay. Leone was grateful and expressed it.

Crushing peanuts in the shade.

During the day we sat around in the shade, holding peanuts between our fingers and smashing them on the ground to extract the nut for fresh eating or using in peanut sauce often served over rice. It was nothing to see neighbors come during the heat of the day to sit under the mango tree for tea. One cup of water was added to a large amount of tea leaves then boiled on top of a wire mesh stand containing hot coals. One quarter cup of sugar was added before the tea was served in tiny cups. Between the sugary tea and the copious amounts of rice consumed, I can understand the diabetes among the natives.

Shade lovers

There were always surprises. The "bush" (forest) may be just a few trees the size of tall bushes. If you didn't watch where you stepped, the undergrowth of vine would trip you. A cashew tree has a fruit about the size of a medium apple with a cashew nut hanging from the bottom. The fruit part is green when first growing, with a thick wall. As the cashew grows, the fruit wall grows thin and leathery as it turns red, indicating the cashew is ripe. The fruit part looks like a red pepper, is chewy and somewhat tasteless, but not consumed. Cashews are considered toxic until blanched, then considered raw.

Cashew fruit

Jean and Andre in bee suits

Andre setting up a hive

I brought bee suits for all three men. Two wooden Langstroth hives were made in Dakar by a woodworker and brought to the Bush. Tires were usually placed under trees and used as a base to hold cement beehives. I wanted to look into a cement hive – the size of a Standard hive – that was placed on top of tires. When the heavy cement top was lifted, the hive rocked, and the bees went crazy. I didn't blame them. I showed the beekeeper how to open the hive, and how to treat the bees. He was surprised at how the bees had settled down and become somewhat tamed. I explained how the hive moving angered the bees. Andre placed his hive under the trees on top of cement blocks rather than tires. Most Africans are afraid of bees, and will burn them if given the chance; as we witnessed during one of our walks into the bush.

Ant hill the height of a man

Andre and I would often walk across the highway from Leone's property into the mango orchard. We would sometimes see huge ant hills about two feet tall, or more. Thankfully, I never saw the ant.

Family of villagers

On our daily walks, we would sometimes meet large families with married children and grandchildren, all living on the same compound. I called them compounds because they would consist of several buildings for residences, kitchen, bedrooms, water well, etc., all fenced in one private area.

White people were not seen in the bush, and I sometimes felt like I was something exotic in a zoo. It was not comfortable with feeling like a strange object being viewed and admired, but the visits usually turned friendly. Often, hugs were given to people when they allowed. Though, I would get concerned whenever a baby or small child cried when they saw my white skin. They must have thought they were seeing a ghost – certainly, something strange.

For me, the silence in the desert always held something other than just the lack of noise. Whenever traveling in different countries, I would often stand in a quiet place away from everyone and the noise and allowed myself to listen and discern what was in the silence. In Africa, the silence held something akin to a very ancient story. Not that it was hiding something, but rather, it would not reveal anything I had not earned the privilege of knowing. In the Nemending bush, I never knew if the cadence of the distant drums I often heard was real, came from an altered reality or was in my imagination. On one occasion, I was told that the lights and drumming were from a festival being held in the next village. It may have been half a mile distance between our compound and the small village, with nothing in between. But the sound and sight so close … I felt like I was there. The sky held very few stars. Even the moon, when it was visible, looked different; like it had been plucked out of somewhere else, and placed in the darkness above me. It almost looked a little out of place in that black, starless sky.

Jean and Andre's family reside in Koalak, where their residence is surrounded by a large wall in the desert without much around them. Koalak, with over a quarter of a million people, is about three hours from Dakar and maybe two hours from Nemending. When I met their mother, I had asked her if I could call her sons my sons. When she asked me why, I responded, "If they say or do something stupid, I can smack them in the back of the head."

She replied, "You are my older sister." And that is how I gained two Senegalese foster sons. I would visit Senegal a few more times over the next few years.

In Africa I understood why I have always had an affinity for the black people. My DNA checked by two different sources, indicates I am 98% Celtic, (60% Irish) and 2% Sub-Saharan (African). As an American, I am called Caucasian – defined as white with European descent. I knew my ancestors were Melungeon, a mixture of Turkish, American Indian, and African. This group of people were born in the Tennessee/North Carolina part of Appalachia mountains and during the 2000-mile march called the Trail of Tears when the Cherokee, Muscogee, Seminole, Chickasaw, and Choctaw nations, and their enslaved Africans, were forced to march to Oklahoma from 1830 to 1840. This march is also referred to as the American genocide of American Indians.[3]

A Melungeon trait is a bump at the back of the skull, which I have. Other traits may be the freckles located elsewhere on the body, other than the face, which I also have. Sometimes there is a gap between the front teeth, and perhaps light-colored eyes. The Scottish part of me was the auburn hair with red highlights before it turned snow white. My eyes are blue with dark blue rings around the outer edges. I am told that this outer ring is the sign of psychic abilities, which I have proven. I had thought everyone can "see" because it is so natural for me.

Revelations into my personality always seemed to surprise me. The one thing my traveling showed me was how easy it was for me to connect and communicate with people. I relished in learning about them, their culture, their desires; literally what made them tick. The more I communicated, the more likeable I became – so I was told. This changed my whole perspective of who I was. Up until then, I thought myself an introvert, but learned I am also an extrovert. I was whatever the situation called for. I found myself immersing in cultures and readily absorbed the new knowledge. I never saw

---

[3] https://en.wikipedia.org/wiki/Trail_of_Tears

living conditions so harsh that I could not adapt, except perhaps in a village on the Lake Albert. Often, I would come back to the States with a slightly changed accent.

During my stay in Senegal, I learned that Jean had gone to school for IT Specialist, and worked in that capacity for several years in his own business as well with another company. Presently, he is in the States, working as an IT man for his friend. Andre sharing how he wanted to be an Architectural/Civil Engineer Technician, I supported him while he attended college for three years, until he graduated in 2015. He now has a business partner and supervises building large commercial structures. I am immensely proud of both of my sons.

A Different Attitude

Arriving back home, things were the same, yet different, as I got busy with different projects and newsletters were written. I went about beekeeping with a different type of gratitude and began teaching more one-on-one students in my bee yard. A group of kids from a summer camp would visit me for a few hours. One day in mid-spring of 2014, I found myself hesitating before entering the apiary next to the Healing Room. For a couple of weeks, I would grab the plastic handle on each of the four barb wire lines used as the entrance gate and hesitated before entering – never knowing why. Then came the day when I touched the last of the four wires and placed it on the fence. I intuited that today would be different. The air around me was electrified, as the hair on my arms stood up. I slowly walked into the apiary and went behind the first beehive to do my inspection. I laid my hand on top of the hive and sent loving thoughts before slowly opening the lid and laying it down on the shelf between the hives. After placing the frame hanger on the edge of the top box, I slowly and carefully inspected each of the first four frames and placed them on the frame hanger. Then it started.

The energy surrounding me slowly changed, creating a bubble with me in the center. I knew I was in the Now alternate state when my consciousness expanded. Looking down on the open hive, I saw the bees *floating* a few inches above the frames; their wings moving in slow-motion. I could actually see each of the four wings move. When I heard the soft music of a trumpet and a harp play a melody I had never heard before, I slowly took one step back away from the hive. I stood there for what seemed like ten minutes, listening to the mesmerizing music and watching the bees slowly waltzing in mid-air to the music's melody. Some of bees' four wings moved in different up-and-down directions, and I was frozen by time by the fascinating view and by the sounds in front of me.

Slowly, the energy shifted again, and I felt my awareness shift with it. My expanded consciousness slowly ebbed as the invisible bubble slowly dissolved. The music silenced as I slowly came out of the altered state. The bees' wings were again beating so fast, I heard the buzzing that had been silent a few moments before. Bees were thumping my head, telling me I had been too long in the open hive. I didn't finish the inspection and put the lid back on. I quietly stood there for a moment, still mentally hearing the music. It was okay because I had always recorded my inspections. I can listen to it later when I transcribe my notes.

After our evening meal, I sat down to my computer with anticipation and turned on the recorder to listen to the inspection. What I thought was ten minutes of music was actually two minutes of silence in between the four-frame inspection and the bees telling me to get out of the hive. Stunned, I replayed the recording again. No voice, no wings, no buzzing, no wind – nothing. I knew then for certain, that the song they played was from the other side – an altered reality. They had taken me into their world and blessed me. Feeling a little disappointed, yet blessed, I got up from my chair and went to clean the kitchen.

I didn't remember any more inspections beyond the first hive that day, though my notes told me I did go into the other hives. All the while, I kept thinking about how they had humbled me to my knees. Kept thinking about learning how to keep my bees by watching them; listening to them; touching them; feeling their healing stings; and receiving their gift of song in an altered state. I honored them with gratitude for sharing their world. They healed my body, cleansed my emotions and mentality. They turned me into a feeling human being. My emotions had been numbed for forty years. It was nice to "feel" again. My personality changed after that altered reality in the bee yard – though I could not have told you when or how. From that day on, the more I was with people, the more I wanted my bees. Bees did not surprise me with their stings as humans always did.

Everything on the earth, because of their atomic movements, vibrates at a certain frequency called Hz (Hertz):

> "The second universal law, the law of vibration, posits that everything (every atom, object, and living thing) is in constant motion, vibrating at a specific frequency. (Regan, June 27, 2021)" [4]

I would learn in 2024 that the buzzing sounds of honeybees affect the hippocampus gland in the brain that stores memories. Bees buzz at the Key of C, which evokes emotions and is the key I resonate with, as most of us do. The buzzing sounds enter your inner ear, then turn into electrical signals that are changed to vibrations. The sound vibrations then travel as signals through the auditory cortex to the amygdala located behind each ear. The signals travel to their final destination, the memory chamber called hippocampus. Some brain areas are used to compare the signals coming from the two ears to figure out from where the sounds come. Other brain areas decode or process language and music. Drums, rain, running water, bee buzz, etc. are all sounds that calm because of their created vibrations.[5]

Sights, smells, tastes and sounds create the memories that can create the physical symptoms of PTSD and are stored in the hippocampus. However, this same process of the senses can also reverse the symptoms. PTSD cannot be cured because one cannot cut out their memories. But there is a way to heal from the symptoms by using sound to put those memories in a place in the brain where you can still see your memories. They just no longer govern your life.

As I traveled, I kept up with creating the newsletters for Kelly Magazine, BEe Healing Guild and the Center for Honeybee Research. Writing was, and still is, a joy that grounds me. There were interviews with beekeepers, scientists, researchers, organizations from all over the world. Looking back on a lot of my writings, I discovered that I didn't spell check, and my editing was not well done as when I read the article I had written for Bee Culture after my Italy trip. Reviewing it years later, I was surprised that it went through without their editing, though I would swear to you at the time that things were fine. I attribute this to PTSD, and how it affects the short-term memory; and not

---

[4] https://www.mindbodygreen.com/articles/law-of-vibration
[5] https://www.myrelaxation.online/healing-frequencies/

being aware of my needing to allow my work to get cold before going back to it.

While in Senegal in January 2014, Patrick had his first bout with kidney issues. My friend was sitting with Patrick when it happened and emailed me, saying it looked serious. Patrick was visiting the doctor, when he was told to go to the hospital. Thirty hours later Carl picked me up at the airport at midnight, and took me to Patrick. My mind had pictured my husband lying in a hospital bed with intravenous lines, oxygen, etc. I was instantly annoyed, when I saw him up and walking around with an IV in his arm. He patted a lounge chair, and said I could sleep there. I informed him I had slept in one for 24 hours and was not sleeping in another. After checking with the nurses, Carl took me home.

Getting Ready

My life took on a pace that kept me going and doing with not enough time to think about much of anything other than beekeeping. In truth, I didn't want to. Looking back on it, I am convinced that I had a feeling of what was coming in the future and didn't want to face it. At the same time, it was like I was racing toward it and wanted it done. In May, 2014 I attended a 3-day conference at the American Apitherapy Society and received my Charles Mraz Apitherapy Course certification.

Me and Dr. Norul Badriah Hassan

In the late spring of 2014, a student from Malaysia – Dr. Norul Badriah Hassan, pharmacologist and Senior researcher, University of Malaysia, School of Medical Sciences – had emailed and asked to stay with me starting August, 2014. She neglected to tell me that Polio had impaired her foot. She walked with a limp, but needed assistance with other things. I had to do a lot of lifting for her during her rare visits to the bee yard where we took pictures of her rather than inspections. I took her to functions, where she glowed at being the center of attention. I was not happy with her wanting me to pay for certain Kosher foods, if I could find them, and not wanting to pay me the small stipend for rent the university had given her me. She was an excellent consumer when she went shopping, but I refused the task of listing all the items she purchased in filling three shipping boxes. She flew back and left me to pack those boxes, anyway, and I arrange for their pickup. I finally realized that I was a convenient trip to America paid by her university.

Patrick on his electric scooter

During all of this, Patrick had his second kidney failure episode. My life got busy in so many directions, with everyone making so many demands on me. No one seemed to notice I was getting weaker. I thought it was just fatigue and overwork. But the day came when I felt the pain in my chest. I angrily told everyone to go to their own corners, and I laid down. I knew then I had to take measures to preserve my own health. I took Norul to the airport before Christmas and assured her that her boxes would arrive in Malasia. She did not return to finish her visit. In January, I resigned as Ambassador for the Center for Honeybee Research. That one hurt, because I so enjoyed the position and the work.

When I tried to place my free colony into their permanent box, I upset the bees when I dropped a frame. Having no protection and stung 19 times, I ran back to the house. Thinking it was a shortcut, I started out walking down the bank, but tripped and slid down the 10' bank to the ground near my back porch. X-rays showed a spiral break in my right leg and was placed in a leg cast. During the 8-week healing period and to the doctor's disbelief, X-rays showed how the venom healed the arthritis in my ankle. The doctor thought he had the wrong x-rays until I told him it was bee venom. He had heard of apitherapy, but that was the first time he had seen it work.

Having proof of Apitherapy and fascinated by the idea of the bees healing the arthritis in my ankle, I began doing my own thing after receiving my Apitherapy Certification. I taught my first Apitherapy Course in January 2015. Students came from across the USA, Canada and Tripoli. I taught two more Apitherapy classes. Eventually, people and their partners came to my healing room and were taught how to sting for Lyme Disease.

My heart issue came to a head when, in February 2015, I had an aortic valve replaced in my heart with an artificial tissue valve. A pacemaker was put in a day later. June of the same year I had a Laminectomy surgery on L2-L5 vertebras in my lower back. I had been using a cane for a while by then and stung my lower back six times twice a week to keep walking. The stenosis never came back, as I was told. But the hips needing replacements kept me on a cane a while longer.

Fall of 2015 was my first Gathering with several well-known speakers from across the US. Classes were held in my Spring Creek Community Center and in the Spring Creek firehouse. Other than a few volunteers disappointing me in their duties and taking advantage, the Gathering was a great success. Many looked forward to the 2016 Gathering that never happened. I couldn't find a venue cheap enough without my going deep into debt. I also didn't want to again be disappointment by the volunteers not following through on their end. I could no longer pick up their tasks. And my hips kept me in pain.

Lady being videotaped

March, 2016, I was contacted by Joe and Terry Graedon, Podcasters for NPR (National Public Radio) to do an interview for the radio program about healing the body using beehive products. That same year, I was contacted by a friend to do a videotape about beekeepers. 2015 and 2016 had many surprises.

I completed and published my book, *Apitherapy, from a BEe Perspective Beekeeper*, in April, 2016. While writing my books, I thought of the places I had traveled, and marveled at how much I had accomplished during my lifetime. Never mind, the amazing people I had encountered. Often, I would think about my life starting at age 65, when I got on my first international plane for Italy. Up until then, it was a matter of getting up, looking on the calendar, and working around it or through it, writing … every day was dull, feeling I was just performing. I was running out of things that fed my mind and soul. But Guidance always comes through.

Entrance to bee bed   Side of bee bed

I designed and built, a portable bee bed on wheels that was completed by August, 2016. It was painted by Matthew Willie, a renowned artist from New York City. His goal was to paint 55,000 giant bees on the buildings of famous enterprises and small businesses. He has made a good business out of it, with a website, www.thegoodofthehive.com. The bee bed was rented once during the gathering. I donated it to another who, after a few years, donated it to another.

She sent me a check for $700. I was much surprised and appreciated it. It paid to have it built.

Dark Days

Patrick started needing my help more and more, keeping me indoors, out of the bee yards, and from traveling. I found myself resenting him. His inability to do some things was another way of my doing for him. In most cases, I refused to go along with it. He stopped caring for himself to the point of only showering once a month. It took a few months for him to admit to me that a lot of it had been due to plain laziness on his part. He also admitted that he had refused knee replacements because of the time he would have had to spend in rehab. Our son took out the bathtub and installed a walk-in all-tiled shower with a seat and a glass front and door. Patrick said he could not maneuver his feet over the 4" hump, but always seemed to manage by holding onto the multiple hand bars. He wanted me to bath him. I didn't do it.

Having worked as a CNA in a nursing home, I saw the signs and recognized the "old man odor." It came from his medication and his body slowly breaking down. As long as he was able to walk indoors, even with the walker, I refused to wait on him. I became a bitch to keep him moving, to keep him alive. He would have me feed him, bath him … anything to keep me home. Then came the day I had had enough.

I walked into his den – where he lived – and told him he had three choices: respite care, nursing home, or someone to come in and care for him. When he asked why, I stated, "I have two grandbabies whom I have not hugged, so I'm going to Africa to hug them." He chose to stay home, and in December 2017, I went to Senegal to hold my grandbabies. While I was gone, a couple of my friends kept him company for a few hours. There were no mishaps or accidents while I was gone. But I intuited it was just the lull before the storm.

When I discovered that he was giving the doctors wrong information, I started going into the examination room with him. He had another kidney episode. After I brought him home, I researched for nursing facilities close to home. I have always had the ability to sense what I needed to do before an event happened. I had not gone into my bees in over a year and was back down to one apiary. Missing their buzzing sounds and their bodies on my arms, I carried a heavy heart.

Because creativity comes from the soul, it always kept me grounded; whether it was basketweaving, loom weaving, painting, or writing – anything artistic. So, I worked on my book, *BEeing Around the World*. Caring for my mother taught me caretaking is not an easy task. So, I did what I could with setting things up for caretaking my husband. Took on more and more tasks around the house. After another kidney episode, I again brought him home, and went through the den closet. Up until then, I felt the den to be off limits. I was stunned to find duplicate prescriptions for needles, glucose strips, etc. filling the shelves. I had asked why so many, he said they kept sending them. I knew it was just a matter of him not remembering what he had, and just said yes to the callers. I cleaned out the den and kept things in labeled boxes, knowing they were going to be donated after his death.

Yes, I knew he was dying. I took on the role of a numbed caretaker and went about doing what I could get done while driving and traveling a lot. I will share that a caretaker will enter, what I have termed to be, a perfunctory state. It is a place of no thought, just doing what is needed, without prioritizing anything. At the beginning of his illness, it would really irritate me that the medical community would not believe me when I told them that Patrick had dementia. So, I would leave the examining room then wait a few minutes for the nurse to come out and tell me the doctors wanted me back in the room. It only happened once with each doctor. I had found the best nursing home 90 minutes away. Getting financial assistance through our local county Human Resources on his income alone, made me glad that we had kept our finances separate.

To qualify for assistance, our savings had to be less than $2000, but we were allowed a vehicle. So, I traded the Nissan in and bought a 2018 Subaru, Forester with our savings. Patrick said nothing after he rode his scooter out to the car, turned around, went back up the ramp and into the house. He was always the one who chose the vehicles in the past, but had no control over the choice of the Subaru. It didn't matter. I was proud to finally get a car I knew I would thoroughly enjoy driving. Still do.

Again, Guidance always steps in when needed. While in the dealership waiting for my car that was being ready for me to take home, I met a woman who was a 30-year veteran in offering assistance for caretakers. She told me that if I just mention the word Hospice, all communication would open up. Goodness ... but she was right!

Separation

While in the hospital room after another kidney episode, Patrick asked when he was going home. The doctor turned to me and said, "Your husband is beyond home care." The doctor explained, and Patrick got angry. His control over me was gone. I then mentioned Hospice to the doctor, and communication did, indeed, open up. The doctor said that they would no longer do exams or tests, as they would do no good. He also said that he may be looking at kidney-dialysis in the future. I informed Patrick that I had found an excellent, top-rated nursing home, with a lot of people he could talk to. That I had visited it already and felt good about it. A few days later, he went by ambulance to the nursing home. His mood had changed, but I couldn't read it.

He did his best to fit in. Looking back over the years, I saw him alone a lot because he never made friends easily, if at all. If he didn't meet them through work, which didn't last long, he had met them through me. There was only one male friend that lasted for several years until he and his wife moved away; I had worked with his wife. Patrick loved telling his stories that grew larger and more extravagant every time he told them. It was his way of trying to be friendly. I also saw where he tried to emulate some of my traits, but they never went over well. The year before his death, his brother and sister came and visited. During the visit, our son drove us back home in our Nissan and sped down the mountain, as he had done with me twice before. Patrick saw that I had not lied, and that Gil had a mean streak.

Except for four days, I traveled the three-hour round trip daily to the nursing home for the 32 days he resided there. Everyone kept telling me to take time for myself. But I knew what they did not. There was a Friday when had I walked into his room, and knew something was wrong. While he was in his wheelchair, I kept pulling on his clothes, until I saw his ankles. It was Friday, the day the doctor did his rounds, so I went looking for him. A few minutes later, he was in Patrick's room. "He needs to go to the hospital. His kidneys are failing." Back to the hospital he went.

After another couple of weeks, the nursing staff became quietly aware of my intuitions and worked with me. When Patrick went back to the nursing home, he knew he would have the catheter for life; and would eventually be on kidney dialysis. The nursing home was large with several wings, consisting of about twenty rooms per wing. I had chosen them, because they also had a hospice facility, which turned out just to be a very large room; but, as it turned out, would not be needed. The head nurse on his wing saw the scar on my shoulder and asked when I had my pacemaker put in. I answered her.

There was one instance that will forever stay in my mind. While I was sitting in the wheelchair (no other chairs were available), Patrick kept staring at me with a distant look I had never seen before. I asked what was wrong, and he slowly moved his head to the right and left. I did not sense anything negative. It was as though he was going over our years together in his mind. I often think back on that moment, and wonder if he wasn't saying his blessings, thank you, or just appreciating. I will never know. We just sat there for about five minutes and stared at each other, before he laid back in his pillow and closed his eyes.

On Monday, October 1st 2018, I picked up my Senegalese son, Jean, and his wife at the airport. We did our touring thing for three days. On Friday, October 5th, we visited Patrick. While driving to the nursing home, the head nurse called, and said Patrick had been given morphine that morning because he could no longer swallow his pills. I knew that swallowing was the last physical ability to go before death. When I arrived, he was partly conscious, but unable to speak. He did squeeze my hand, when I spoke to him. We both knew.

My few tears fell as Jean and Cissy silently sat in their chairs, not knowing what to say or do. They did shake his hand, when I introduced them and said a few words. When Patrick closed his eyes and no longer squeezed my hand, I placed his bi-pap machine in his wheelchair, and the three of us went out the door. It felt surreal when pushing the wheelchair past the nursing station and everyone staring at me.

We left before noon and went grocery shopping on the way home, arriving at the house at 2:50 PM. At 3:10 PM the nurse called, and informed me Patrick had passed at 3:00 PM. She related that she and another nurse chanted, as he passed over. I went back about two weeks later and brought a flower arrangement for the staff of the wing. I gave them to the head nurse of his wing and explained, that I was always there because, being an intuit, I knew his time was short. She informed me that the whole nursing staff was very aware of my intuitive abilities. Neither of us said anything more. It would not be until several weeks later that I would wonder if they had given him an extra dose of morphine.

Grieving

The next two weeks were spent entertaining Jean and Cissy. Torn between depression, sadness and anger at Cissy for insisting on cleaning my house, I had the additional burden of guilt for Cissy taking away my friend's cleaning business, who badly needed the money. It didn't occur to me to just give her the money; and just accept that Cissy was doing for an elder and her mother, as is Senegalese custom. I just remained angry and didn't really understand why at the time. I feel it was because I was thinking back over the 53 plus years being married to a manipulative Italian, who had a lot of insecurities and fears. Then, that was when it hit me.

In the beginning of our marriage, Patrick ruled. He held the checkbook, and made the major decisions. He pretty much did what he wanted, because he was head of the house. As the years passed, my insecurities fell away. My social skills became stronger when I continued observing and listening to others while among people. And I watched Patrick. I was free to do this, because he was there to take care of me, right? Well, that changed over time. The more I learned, the stronger I got, the more Patrick let go. I learned to take care of myself. His weaknesses made me stronger.

After we had moved to Frederick, I built my first woodshop in our garage. Even I was surprised how much I was able to do. And it seemed to come naturally. I no longer question it; accepted it. If I wanted to do something, I just did it. Then I remembered the voice I had heard while lying in bed when I was four years old. "Lady, you can do anything." I realized I had married Patrick because of his supporting me through my painful times as I grew during our marriage. We had reversed roles long before he died.

Four days after Patrick's death I posted it on Facebook. I had forgotten I was "friends" with Gil on Facebook. The daughter of Gil's partner posted, "Do you not remember telling Patrick that you wished he would die?" I was stunned and totally blown away. I had no idea from where that came. She had visited us once in the five years I had known her. My friends on Facebook defended me, and that was enough for me to block her, her mother, and Gil from Facebook, email, Messenger, and my cell phone. I was hurt to think anyone would think I could say such a thing about anyone – never mind my husband.

I had already cleaned out part of Patrick's clothing and his Den. There was not much more to do. A week after taking my guests to the airport, I researched for retreats near me and found one about an hour's drive from home. The week at the retreat was spent doing a little gym workout, meditation, a couple of massages, and participating in the evening talks. I was the oldest and, supposedly, the wisest. A role I slowly accepted for what it was; someone who had experienced a lot of painful lessons and life.

The Keto diet was another element the retreat also gave me. It regulated my diabetes that came from PCOS (Poly Cystic Ovary Syndrome). Ironically, it was my cardiologist who found the condition. At the time, the medical community still didn't know what caused PCOS. The hormones, Testosterone, androstenedione or LH.[6] is found in 86% of the women with PCOS. And I am one of them. I was told that PCOS came about because of the stress of sexual assaults and abuse that creates hormonal conditions. Research indicates that the condition stems from the mother being stressed during the first trimester, affecting the DNA in the embryo.[7] Mom was greatly stressed when pregnant with me.

PCOS created a barrel torso; a deeper voice; hair growth on my body, especially the face. I also had a large number of testosterones that created stronger muscles. At 76, I pushed a 42" riding mower up a slight incline, up the ramp, and onto the trailer. When I said that, a man standing alongside me said he couldn't do that. I, alone, pushed a Ford truck out of mud. The Keto diet also increased my libido, like I had never experienced before.

I had kept writing my book, *Apitherapy – from a BEe Perspective Beekeeper,* while caretaking my husband. It was published in January 2019, by Peace Publishers, my publishing company. At the end of January 2019, I received a WhatsApp text message on my phone from Gil. He had never called to say he was sad his dad had died. Nor had he ever called asking how I was doing – nothing. He texted that he his new phone came with the app and wanted to text me. That was it – nothing else.

I texted back something similar to: "When you were in the Navy or traveled, you stayed away a long time without ever calling home to see how we were doing or to update us on your news. I do thank you though for going down the mountain at breakneck speed with your aunt and uncle in the back seat.

---

[6] https://pubmed.ncbi.nlm.nih.gov/1296589/
[7] https://www.ncbi.nlm.nih.gov/pmc/articles/PMC4499527/

Your father never believed me when I told him that you had done that to me twice before. I respectfully request you continue your silence. I am tired of the disrespect and abuse. I wish you well." Then I blocked his number.

A couple months later, while driving to town, I saw Gil in a different truck as he passed me on the mountain. When I got to the restaurant, I waited to see if he would come in. I never heard from him again. I sometimes wondered about him, and on rare occasions would think of reconnecting with him. But the thought quickly passed. I am certain he and his partner and daughter have spread rumors that made me out the bitch. His MO was getting pity any way he could, while taking on the role of a martyr. I could not do anything about the sixteen years of abuse he received before he came to us as a foster child. We did what we could in the near forty years we had him, and supported him through his suicide attempts and five marriages. I had nothing more to give him. There were times I regretted adopting foster children. Yet, I knew that had it not been for us, they would have suffered a great deal more without our love and teachings. But it was now time for me.

A New Me

It took a year to grieve Patrick. I remembered receiving a letter from hospice when mom died about not selling anything major or signing any paperwork for at least a year after her death – preferably two years. I understood why. Your brain is not with you all the time. Sometimes, it could be anywhere else or nowhere in particular – just blank. It is just there, waiting for who knew what. Sometimes I would think about things. Like why Patrick always wanted me to call Gil for work around the house when I wanted to call another handyman; it eventually occurred to me. Patrick gave Gil a lot of money for gambling, food, chauffeuring him to the casino. Having him work around the homestead, was his way of getting his money back. Patrick maintained his Jewish mentality to the end.

Also, during the year of grieving, I met a man online whom I later learned was an internet romancer. I confess to being naïve and vulnerable enough to send him $5,000. A little voice within me mentioned research, and I did. The house on his site was found in California. I noticed other discrepancies in his texts. It was like a light bulb had turned on in my head. I had also kept the email he sent me. As a professional executive secretary, we never throw away any communications. We just file it, because you never know when you will need it. I went on my sister's Facebook and found the same person. I texted her, and we had a conversation. At the time, I had been with Edward Jones Investment Firm. I went to them about the $5,000, and they contacted their fraud department. They also gave me a stern lecture for having sent it and would have talked me out of it had they known. During my conversation with the investigator, I gave him the impersonator's name and email. After a few moments of phone silence, he said, "We have him!" When I asked what they were going to do with the information I gave them, he said that it would be given to the FBI and Scotland Yard. About six months later I saw a news report on the internet about 81 international internet romancers being arrested. I like to think my $5,000 went towards part of that investigation.

In the same year, I learned about myself. I had married and stayed with a manipulator who tried to keep me from my friends. The longer we were married, the less I knew we had in common. Thinking back on it, I think I may have married him to get out of mom's house. I sat for a year and thought about my 53+ years with a man I had only known for three months before marriage. I loved horses, and he said he did, too. After we went to a horse ranch to ride, he said he was afraid of them. I made a mental note of his lie. He waited in the car while I rode. He enjoyed bowling; I tried that for about ten years. He enjoyed golf; I tried that for a few years. Ironically, I was good at all the sports. Toward the end of the marriage, I stayed outside in the gardens more; while he stayed in his den. During my grieving time, I realized that I had fallen out of love with him twenty years before, which is why I looked for things outside of the home away from him.

What I found curious is that every time I called him on the things he did or said to me, he would claim no memory of it. Manipulators will deny telling lies. I had forgotten that information about abusers; something I learned while manager of a safe house. In time, we just stopped communicating. One thing that did come out of the marriage is that every time he displayed a weakness, I took it up and got stronger. Over time, I took over a lot of the things he had done. He did all the lawn mowing with a walking mower. But I operated the riding mower because I think he was afraid of it. The PCOS made me physically strong, so I even surpassed him on that. In truth, I think he just gradually gave up on a lot of things. One night, while we were in bed, he did say that if one of us had to die first, he wanted it to be him. That he could not take care of me like I took care of him. That was evident from the beginning. I am convinced we were together so that I could grow strong and confident.

I sold the house and property in the August 2019. Money never meant to me what it does to others. I never wanted it when I didn't have it, and gave it away when I received it. The house sold for what I had put into it, including all repairs, additions, etc. Keeping all the receipts in an expenditure journal was an occupational hazard. I never regretted selling the house; nor for the amount it sold – I was never greedy. Though I did love the area and got along well with the community, there was nothing there for me anymore. I had hired a lawn maintenance man to take care of the yard that last year before the sale. Not having had a mortgage, I divided the house money between my two Senegalese sons and a third for me. Gil received nothing. We had sold him our Dome in Sneedville for $47k when it was worth over $200k – that was his inheritance. A 2-bedroom apartment on the ground floor in Asheville, NC, was my next move.

Dolphins are one of my favorite mammals, and was my great desire to swim with them after seeing movies on how human-friendly they were. In October 2019, I lectured at a Florida State Bee Meeting, and my speech payment was room and board with a Dolphin package. After swimming and interacting with the dolphins, they were removed from my bucket list.

Curious thing, during the Florida State Bee Meeting, a representative for a company selling probiotics to honeybees attended my lecture on honeybees and good bacteria. I included my Lacto-formula. I made sure I stressed adding *L. casei* to the formula, because the bacterium because I had seen that it was not listed in the company's ingredients. I started the lecture with my formula because I thought they needed to know how it was in all living things on the earth, including in the earth. I don't know if they took the suggestion.

Japan, Senegal & Uganda

Yumiko's family

In the first part of December 2019, I went to Japan for their first Annual Honeybee Conference. Japan from the air is a sight to see with all the property outlined in precise square plots. Their breakfast buffets are intriguing with seaweed and raw egg. Thinking it was a boiled egg with the intentions of peeling it, I cracked it and made a mess. Considering the number of diners in the dining room, I was impressed how quiet it was.

Their conference was elaborately set up on the first two floors of a beautiful building with a lot of room between vendors. Yumiko's family are a third generation of beekeepers, and they were very active on the ground floor selling bee products. Yumiko introduced me to her husband and sons while spending as much time as she could with me. On Saturday night, everyone went to the liquor bar. Social hour was really quiet – until the foreigners came in. Then you couldn't hear the person next to you. Did I mention that their toilet water system was a major engineering design. Too bad, I was not an engineer. And such tiny rooms in the hotel.

Me on a camel

The next three weeks were spent in Senegal, Africa, visiting family. For the first time in many trips, Andre arranged for us to actually tour Dakar. He surprised me with the experience of riding a camel. What shocked me more was his lifting me up onto the camel, my butt being at his shoulder height, and placed me in the saddle. When we finished the ride, he lifted me off the saddle. The African sun makes strong bones, and manual labor makes strong muscles. He once walked a mile with a hundred-pound bag of stone balanced on his head. Placing a twisted handkerchief, formed into a circle, balanced the bag on his head. We also visited Africa's new and only African museum, advertised as the largest in the world. It was expansive as it told of Africa's history. It also contained history of other parts of the world, including Native American Indians.

Gori Island, located off the coast in Atlantic Ocean, is where the African slaves were taken and shipped to the new world. I didn't want to go to Gori Island because I knew of my ability to see and hear spirits. Besides, according to my DNA, one of my ancestors was an African slave from Camaroon in southwestern part of Africa. I am proud of my heritage – but slavery? I couldn't go there because I knew I would feel it.

A couple of months before my move to my apartment, I was contacted by Nashif Amed, a participant of the International Apitherapy Forum and a native in Uganda, Africa. We had texted for quite a while. After feeling I could somewhat trust him, I made arrangements to visit him to teach beekeeping. He volunteered to be my host, so on February 2020, after

Senegal, I flew to Uganda. I was picked up at the Entebbe airport by Nashif and his friend Asaba Ramathan, to whom I was immediately drawn. Nashif was amiable. But when we arrived at his house, I discovered that he had spent the $900 I sent for my visit, on items for himself. When I mentioned it, he just smiled and said, "Oh, yeah." My first red flag of many to come. Asaba didn't speak much English, but smiled frequently. My attraction to him perplexed me. He was nice looking, but I found I was drawn to him on a deeper level. "I have a wife," he responded when I asked if he dated.

Always traveling with one foot in the spirit world and the other in this reality. I often wondered if the downside of my relying a lot on Guidance was my missing some of the little things that I should have paid attention to. I had allowed Nashif to use my debit card. He was allowed to keep the unspent funds, but I had to continually explain that the funds in the account were not mine, that I would have to replace what we spent. He said nothing. Another red flag. At this point, I was wondering why I didn't do the withdrawing of funds myself, but still was not compelled to do so. I wanted very much to make a difference, and thought I was doing so by helping someone in a poor community. There was something nagging at me on a daily basis, but I could not pin it down. I waited.

Bridge over Nile River

Lake Victoria is Africa's largest lake and the beginning source of the Nile River, fed by a large natural spring continually bubbling up in the lake. The river flows northward and empties into the Mediterranean Sea, more than 6,600 kilometers (4,100 miles) to the north, making it one of the longest rivers in the world. When the three of us walked across the bridge over the Nile River, I felt a very strong energy cord move from Asaba's hand flow through my right hand into my core. This was the first time I experienced such a thing, and it touched me on a level I cannot describe. Asaba was the one who held my hand every time the three of us were together. I knew Nashif was always off somewhere bragging about having a white woman with him. Another red flag. I was beginning to question my mentality in not doing something about it. But I was still not compelled.

Me and Asaba on the Nile

Always being a daring adventurer, I took off my outer clothes and bathed in the Nile. In nearly every picture taken in Uganda, Asaba and I were touching hands, arms, or shoulders – something. Whenever he was near, his energy felt good. The one time we were not touching was when we were in a boat with life jackets while sitting next to each other with gentle smiles on our faces.

Giraff in the Savannah

We drove through the Queen Elizabeth National Park, with a guide in the car sharing information about the savanna. Monkeys were everywhere. The roaming giraffes and rhinos were fascinating while watching them move in slow motion. Everything was like in the movies or pictures – the short trees, open spaces, occasional hut or small village. There were times, I felt like was dreaming or had stepped onto another world.

We also visited a village that had no inside or outside toilets, anywhere. When I had asked about the round pellets I was stepping on, I was told the villagers would squat where they were and defecated on the sand. Lake Albert was the only source of water for laundry, bathing, drinking, and fishing for the villagers. I noticed the sores on many heads, and knew the source of infection was from the contaminated lake water. Fish and rice were their main diet. We watched a couple of men repair a large fishing net that was used to toss out into the lake from a boat. I had never seen poverty on this level. What impressed, confused, and irritated me, all at the same time, was that nearly everyone had a cell phone.

One of our trips included the sacred hot springs, and we brought along Richard, another one of Nashif's friends. Though I wondered about that, after hearing Nashif speak to him like a lowly servant. Some places in the hot springs were just puddles in the ground, but the whole thing ran like a shallow, narrow stream. And the water temperature was like hot bath water. No vehicles were allowed in the area, so Nashif and I rode on a rented motorcycle from the parking lot to the hot springs, or walked part of the way. While sitting on a stone next to the springs, I watched Asaba walk toward us down the steep road, holding onto his yellow shirt while talking to Richard. I watched how his foot gently stepped on the earth, and how his body gently moved. My heart suddenly skipped a beat, and for a hair-breath's moment, I thought I was having a heart issue. My heart softened as he neared us with a smile on his face. No other man, including my husband, had ever made me feel that way.

I wanted to experience the benefits of the springs, so I undressed down to only my panties and sat down next to a large rock in the water. Asaba walked over and sat on the large rock to watch me from above. It seemed so natural to have him close like that. He was the one who held my hand, watched over me, put my shoes on. He literally took care of me and nurtured me whenever he was with us. It felt so familiar that it almost made my uneasy.

Nashif received permission to drive to the other side of the hot springs to take a shorter trip home. When we got to the edge of the springs, we had slowed down to cross a tiny stream running from Lake Albert. Two men appeared out of nowhere. One standing in front of our vehicle but across the stream with legs apart and holding a bat in one hand and using the tip to hit the palm of his other hand. Another man suddenly appeared on my side just standing there. In Uganda, the driver sat in the right side of the car and drove on the left side of the road. The man looked at me and demanded money. I looked to Nashif, who had started whimpering like a baby, with an infant-like expression on his face. It angered me and I looked back to the man. In a very firm, strong voice, said, "Hell no." He just stared at me in disbelief then waved off his companion, who moved to one side of the road with a confused look on his face.

Neither Nashif nor I said anything while he stared straight ahead and drove through the water, up to the top of the dirt road and picked up Asaba and Richard. I had no idea how they got there. I was tiring of this weak person, whom I knew lied to me all the time. He was showing me off like a prized trophy and bragging on himself. He was very much a narcistic individual as I learned that he tries to get others to do his job while he takes the credit. He didn't really act like he wanted to learn about bees or apitherapy, and I began to wonder if we were not connected for the sole purpose of my meeting Asaba. I learned how Ugandan's thought all white people were rich, and Nashif wanted a sugar mama.

Me and Asaba

We went to a night club, but I didn't stay long and went back downstairs. I never could handle the noise of such places; but we did have dinner on the rooftop of the same club. The rest of the three weeks was spent being introduced to people. I did arrange with Nashif to send him to veterinary school. I knew I had left him with enough money to support himself for a while and to get supplies for his veterinary practice. After I came back to the States, I also paid for a motorcycle for him. Nashif texted me that Asaba cried on the way home from the airport after dropping me off. And that Asaba would be texting me after he learned English. Asaba never asked for a thing. But I did purchase a cell phone for him before I left.

I left Uganda at the end of March, 2020, but stayed on the Doxycycline for a month; which is required when traveling to third world countries. The first of March, Jean, now living in USA, visited me and brought Covid with him. He was not ill, but, goodness, did I get sick. I was surprised, because I usually don't get sick. It lasted three weeks during which time I lost my sense of smell, taste, hearing, and my sight blurred, even with glasses.

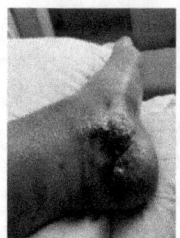

Having neuropathy, my feet are numb so I was unaware of the tiny cut in the bottom of my left foot while in Uganda. After I was back in the States, I would learn of my near fatal mistake of wading barefoot in the water where people had defecated. By April 5th, I was hospitalized for five days with an infection in my whole left leg. The internist told me, that the blood test indicated it was *Enterococcus faecalis*, a bacterium from feces. It could have come from any source – the Nile River, the sacred hot springs, the toilet rooms…. What I do know is that it entered my body through the tiny cut on my foot. When I came back to the States, the Womb Care Nurse, while in ER, cut out the infection at the original sight on my left foot. Honey was used to cover the two large blood blisters on my ankle. Four days later, the blisters fell away, leaving behind new skin.

The internist told me the bugs were dead, but they still did their work after I left the hospital and went sepsis on me. They went through my whole body: For two months, I could not control my bladder; two months of no bowel control; two months of respiratory issues; two months of muscle issues; fatigue during the entire process. It finally hit my heart January 28, 2021. I had a 90-second v-tac (ventricular tachycardia) episode at 2:30 AM. I arose from my bed in the morning and was shocked to find I had voided both my bowels and bladder. I took a shower and changed my sheets. At 11:00 AM, my cardiologist's office called because my heart monitor had sent a message from my pacemaker. My cleaning lady walked into the apartment just at the time I was on the phone. The nurse strongly suggested I go to the ER; before I left my apartment, a room had been booked in Mission Heart Hospital.

I can still remember the ER Cardiologist's face. He never took his eyes off me while questioning and examining me, even after the nurse walked into the room. I will learn a year later those patients with my kind of v-tac episode either stayed sick or died. I did neither. I didn't even look ill. My heart improved and came back to normal in eighteen months. That was unheard of. In February 1, 2021, a defibrillator replaced my pacemaker. It has gone off twice in two years, but I never felt it. When I learned of the dates, I remembered the stress during those times. Since then, I have done my best to stay stress free. I suspect the valve replacement in 2015 is the reason I could no longer move too fast without being out of breath. It seems that the fascia tissue created after any surgery adheres to surgical scars and prevents surrounding muscles from doing their job. This is something the medical society does not explain, but Physical Therapists do.

I supported Nashif for several months in 2020, until I became suspicious for his request for Glaucoma surgery and did some research. I received an email from an eye doctor from the University Hospital, that eye surgery was $500, not the $5,000 Nashif requested. The doctor explained that every patient receives documents explaining the cost of the surgery. Three times, I had asked for a photo of the last page of the receipt that show the surgery cost. I explained on the third attempt that I would block him if he didn't reply to my request. No response came, so he was blocked from all of our social contacts. But I would learn how much trouble he could be.

Something Different

Asaba bought a book on the English language and learned enough to start texting me by mid-April. The more we texted, the more English he understood; and the texting improved. Learning my naivete from Nashif, I was not sure about Asaba. I put him through his paces during our texts – more than once. I was hard with my questions. Sometimes, he took his time. But he always responded. I now know, that he took his time to use what he thought was correct English. However, though he could read and write English, he didn't know how to use it properly. It made for a lot of miscommunications, that forced me to put him through a lot of Q&As during the next three years.

In August 2021, my right hip was replaced with a Titanium. About this time, I mentioned to Asaba that I had feelings towards him. Suddenly, all communications opened up. Until then, he pretty much kept things to himself. In the same month, a Watchman was installed in my heart. This device plugged the heart chamber that creates blood clots that can travel to the brain and other parts of the heart or lungs. My Cardiologist told me that cases like mine were prone to blood clots, so it made me a good candidate. The device had been on the market for only a year. So far, so good.

The bacterium infection I picked up in Uganda had weakened my bladder, and in April 2022, I had a bladder support mesh inserted. September 2022, my left hip was replaced with Titanium. Since before 2015, and before my back surgery of July 2017, I had used a cane. I was on the cane again, until two weeks after each hip surgery. Imagine walking without a cane on my own two legs in 2022. I was told that my left leg was nearly a half inch shorter than my right, and the doctor made up for it by adding it to my hip. When I stood alone for the first time, I chuckled at wanting to lean over to my right. It took a while to get to get use to the idea of actually standing straight.

My friend Ethel had spent the latter part of 2020 and the beginning of 2021 cleaning up after my bowel and bladder messes. One could not ask for a better friend, and who is still with me. While all of this was going on, I kept asking, "Why me?" An unusual question for me since I generally accepted anything that came along.

Ethel

Asaba and I had texted all the while this was going on, and I wondered if I was losing it or had become a dirty old lady. But then, I also thought of all the young people coming into my life as I aged. Some were intrigued, some wanting advice or counseling, and others wanting to just hang out. And I often wondered about nearly all of the men in my life being in their 30's or 40's. It seemed the older I got, the younger my companions became. I also reminded myself that women at 42 and men at 45, thereabouts, stopped growing up and started expanding their brain. Even at 82 years of age, I don't feel older than 45.

Asaba Ramathan

I had been sending Asaba money for his school and helping him build a home for him and his children. When he went to the children's mother and told her about the house, she wanted to squander the money rather than build a home. They parted ways. By Christmas 2021, Asaba and I had become close and started making plans to marry. By the way, did I mention he is 31 in his photo. I could still hear his voice, feel his hand in mine. Always in my mind was watching him walking down the steep road in the sacred hot springs area. Plans for me to fly to Uganda for our marriage kept falling apart. At first, I was confused and upset. Was he scamming me like everyone thought?

During this time, I was content in my first apartment for a couple of years. But their computer issues for autopay kept dropping my info. One day I found a note on the cement walkway just outside my door stating I had thirty days to move out. I got emotional and took the letter to the office manager and told her I was taking her offer to move out. I went online and left a review relating my experiences with the manager of the apartment complex. I later learned the office manager was no longer working there. In the meantime, I had no idea how hard it would be to try to find another place. So, I moved in with my friend for about three months before moving into new apartments that would be ready in August 2021. October was my move-in date. It was not long before I discerned that the complex catered to dogs more than humans. Very few children had lived there and were rarely seen or heard. But the dogs were. There were more than dog problems with them barking, defecating next to my patio, and fighting outside my bedroom. The ceilings were nine feet high, making for costly electric bills in winter with the vents at ceiling height. And the noise bouncing and resonating off the exterior walls of the outside entryway … I was not resting. In July 2022, I moved and in with a good friend, at her son's request because she was struggling with memory issues. All of my possessions were stored on her property.

Still Learning

At the end of three months with my friend, her children went to the place of fear. I felt the energy shift on Monday and questioned her about what her son would say about the check she had insisted on giving to me. I wrote her a post-dated check for three days later, and she was confident it would be okay. Well, it wasn't. Her son made arrangements to pick her up three days later on Friday for her to stay with them at his home. I waited.

Saturday, her daughter texted me at midnight that she needed to come into the house. I didn't understand why she didn't have a key, but I let her in. The next morning, I went out into the living room at 7 AM and asked what was going on. She said, "We want you out. Now." I already knew it was coming. My car was packed within an hour, with her help. My friend never knew what had happened until she came back home after Thanksgiving. Three days after I had moved out, David, another friend helped me get my things out of the garage, with a police escort. When leaving, the deputy related that the property owner told him I would be arrested if I showed up on the property. My friend had forgotten that her son had a Power of Attorney.

Genia, my best friend, helped me to locate a place where I stayed for a month. I floated around for a couple more months until David took me into his spare room for three months. I moved into an apartment in May 2023. It is quiet, beautifully landscaped; and is one of the many original motels Colonel Sanders had built before WWII. There were seven other younger male tenants who kept to themselves, but were friendly and helpful when I needed assistance. NO PETS. I renewed my lease for another year. The building being that old and the floor on the verge of dropping, I did not know that I was developing mold infection.

During all of this, I could see in Asaba's selfies that he had grown since our first meeting in January 2020. Seeing the photos he accidently sent me showing before and after of the bodies of cars he had repaired, I knew him to be very intelligent and very talented in repairing vehicles. He shared that he wanted to be the best mechanic in Uganda. I was going to do my best to see that happened, along with paying for the two children's school tuition. I continually stressed the importance of the children's education. Because his father felt he was better suited in the fields with the cattle, he never went to school. Asaba has come to understand the importance of an education, while he was in mechanic school.

In 2024, it became too dangerous for me to travel to Uganda, so, we started working on getting him here. Two thugs were hired to damage our property and truck. They had beaten our property manager severely enough to put him into the hospital for surgery. They caught Asaba on his motorcycle, severely beat him and gave him a compound fracture and a second break in the same right leg. Though there were witnesses, one thug was put in jail, but was bailed out with no case filed. I expect the witnesses were threatened. Or the police didn't bother, since I would not give them money. I am confident the thugs are waiting for me. Ugandans, including doctors, worship money over anything else – some even over life.

PART VIII
Am I Done?

Who AM I

At 82 years of age, I wonder at what I have learned. I would think a lot, yet, very little – almost all at the same time. People say I am Owl woman, a woman of wisdom. That is true. But I know it comes from the experiences of understanding people, compassion through pain, acceptance and letting go and allowing Universal Guidance.

Age 45, Corporate World

In dealing with a lifetime of abuse, I thought I had become emotionally passive or calloused. I would experience the trauma, not get angry, turn my back on it and go onto something else. I am not sure when this trait had developed or why, but it has served me well. I have learned to view scenarios and issues from the back end, through cracks, windows, back doors by looking through or into things, rather than straight at or to them. This trait allowed me to see into reality, be it a puzzle, an emotion, or acts of others…. It actually helped me survive my personal reality and the working world.

What did surprise me was my ability to feel the emotions of others, have empathy for them, but could not feel for myself. That is, until I found my self-worth. When I was eleven years old standing before granny, I had closed that door on self-love. As an adult there came a day, when I walked into a store, and a man smiled and nodded at me. Then, and only then, did I realized I had been keeping my eyes down. The honeybees' buzzing sounds resonating with my core, eventually opened that door to a place where I can put my painful memories. This is what I mean when I say the honeybees taught me my humanity. They showed me how to let go and be the ageless, multi-faceted being I am today. And Asaba reminded me that we are mentally and emotionally ageless. My emotions for him are unlike any other I have had for any man, including my husband. I know I found a caretaker as much as I have found someone to love me without wanting a nurturer himself; though I know he will care for me when the time comes.

My sensitivity to energies, people, sensations of feelings, etc., could also be the reason I feel so deeply for others; and why I cannot cry for myself when kept in a protective bubble. I don't forgive, but accept. Forgiving for a deed done or a word said is to put myself in a judgement mode. It is Guidance's place to judge. Not mine. Accepting without judgement allows others to change and grow. But I also have the choice of whether or not to allow someone in my personal space or life. Part of my thoughts on what money does to people came from a fight about a dollar between me and mom when I was about thirteen. I wanted to see *South Pacific;* a movie I had already seen five times. Mom said she only had one dollar, but we fought and I ended up slapping her because of my desperation of needing to leave the house and escape. I felt so bad, I ran upstairs and cried. She followed me a few minutes later and gave me her last dollar. I went to the movies. It would be ten years before she allowed me to pay back the one dollar. I think my stubbornness came from my mother.

I have also seen what money can do to other people. In my lifetime, the money I gave often did make a difference where words of wisdom, or acts of deeds, were not enough. People took advantage, I know. But I still kept giving. In truth, I don't regret the money nor the people "using" me. You cannot use someone without their permission. My left-sided thinking always had me feeling sad for those who felt the need to deceive me because I knew they were hurting in their own way.

There were many times, when hurting, I would meditate to that safe place within. When I first began meditating, the instructor would say to go the "center." They would not really answer when I asked the center was. Going on my own, I learned to go within, let go of thoughts and emotions and just allow. First my mind would be dark and empty, then there would be light. No images at all, just light similar to stepping on a white 3D canvas with nothing on it and just meditated; not knowing what to expect. Eventually, it turned to soft white clouds that moved ever so slowly about me. It was during those types of meditations; I came emotionally healed. One time, I had asked Guidance to "show" me where that place was. I meditated to the light and found myself enclosed in a transparent, coffin-like chamber supported by one transparent pedestal. Never did see what I would describe as a floor. There was an entity standing over the slender chamber – no actual shape – just a tall mass of energy. I made me nervous and never saw it again. But it never felt negative. Just did not understand what went on and didn't question it again.

Living Well

Lady at 63, author of first book

It took a lifetime dealing with childhood and military traumas to be at peace and to learn self-love. Having the life tools during childhood would have helped a lot. Being told by my family that I was loved and given hugs would have helped me build courage, given me strength. Eventually, internal peace developed as I fearlessly faced my biggest hurdles: limitations, fears, and the feelings of inadequacy and insecurities. Not knowing what to do, or how to gain the courage to deal with things were my major weaknesses and took the longest to develop. The biggest lessons were watching and listening to others; and gaining the courage to look ridiculous in searching my own emotional strength. An angry person is viewed as someone having "lost it." I don't know if it was anger when I "lost it" twice in my life. But I do now believe that the black button was turned on when people made comments that hit my core belief regarding respect. There was so much crammed down and packed away in my emotional chamber, the black button was a release valve.

My demeaner now is soft. Respect and love are given to me on a global level by beekeepers and professionals alike, and this humbles me. Perhaps, it's because I no longer have expectations. I had them in the past, not of myself, but of others and was often disappointed. I stopped counting on others and went more to the internet. I was in the mountains just doing what I love and sharing it on the internet, with my local community, and all those who would have it. I am very transparent and loath liars. I will oust anyone who lies to me. People are not afraid of me, but are wary of what I may say. Any communication boundaries I may have had were put to the wayside a long time ago. Some call it age. I call it lessons learned. I admire those who can stand up to me and look me in the eye.

Opinions, politics, and religions are subjective, so I don't discuss them or give advice on them. Thought rarely, what I may share is what I have experienced. Even when teaching or lecturing, the first thing I say is: "I don't want you to believe anything I say. But I do suggest that you just listen, file away what you wish to keep and toss the rest. If you have questions, ask me or research it for yourself. What I teach is what I know, and can back it up with studies or experiences. You need to satisfy your own truths."

In the past seven years, I have been contacted by people from my past, so this told me that it is time to come back out of seclusion. I have reconnected with the Center for Honeybee Research to get involved again, and have contacted others. I have even started going out for luncheons. Andre and I talked about his coming to the US to care for me as I age and have expressed that Asaba would take care of me after we marry. But I think I have come to the conclusion that I need to do part of that job myself. Though, I do view Asaba as Guidance's gift to me for my elder years. He loves me for me and not for what I can do for him or give him; and coming from a man, that is a novel.

Allowing and accepting has allowed me to have children all over the world obtained through the internet. There were times when I wondered about my not having my own children. But would remember that we don't really have control over our lives, that we choose our births and deaths before our birth. We even choose the place and the family into whom we are born and will live, solely for the purpose of the lessons in that life. As imperfect beings, all lessons, when learned, teach us the elements of being human that allow our souls to grow toward the state of grace – the path to wisdom and God.

Do you remember that mule I spoke of in the Introduction. It often kicked me; was hard to ride because of going around or over obstacles in the road of my life's journey; and was often hard to understand and communicate with? And, yes, I got off many times and walked alongside it. What I learned from writing *My Life's Crazy Quilt* was that mule and I have been together my entire life and just didn't know it. The Dual University has two opposing sides, even in our own personalities. You see, I *am* that mule. We still have our differences, but we have learned to get along and to love each other. I am at peace.

Know you are loved.

www.ingramcontent.com/pod-product-compliance
Lightning Source LLC
Chambersburg PA
CBHW051943290426
44110CB00015B/2088